RURAL MINISTRY
and the
CHANGING
COMMUNITY

RURAL MINISTRY
and the
CHANGING
COMMUNITY

Rockwell C. Smith

ABINGDON PRESS Nashville and New York

To Frances
my wife
in whose companionship the rural ministry is joyful

Preface

Social scientists and religious professionals are aware of how much their work depends upon the labors of other human beings, men not only currently alive and at work, but men of the near and distant past as well. The author, both a sociologist and a minister, is doubly aware of his debt. Beyond the general indebtedness all such professionals own, his is a particular and specific one. Over two hundred rural sociologists and over three hundred town and country Methodist pastors have joined in providing the materials and the outline out of which this book has grown. Without these colleagues and friends, this presentation could not have existed.

The sociologists gave their judgments as to what materials within the context of rural sociology would be of major importance in equipping the town and

7

country pastor for his leadership role within the rural community. The ten concepts treatment, which constitutes chapters 4 through 13, is a distillation from the substance of their professional discipline. Presumably professors know better than any other category of persons that discipline and the rural community it studies; their understanding of the role the pastor plays may not reflect the same expertise, but they certainly have a sophisticated layman's comprehension of that role.

The ministers, chosen to represent town and country pastors in the Methodist Church, provided a measure of the degree of understanding pastors possess of the materials of rural sociology and also a measure of performance characteristics of Methodist pastors in their churches and in the communities those churches serve. Their replies demonstrated that sociological know-how is positively related to church programs which reach out to serve the community, and that churches so engaged are more healthy in the measures of institutional maintenance than churches which have little to do with the communities in which they exist. It does in fact make a real difference in community and church if the minister serves with some sociological knowledge of community and group process.

Though the focus of particular concern in this text is the pastor and his role in the community, the treatment has relevance for such other community servants as the farm adviser, the home adviser, the school administrator, the teacher, the politician, and the professional man who seeks to take the lead in helpful community change. The people whose community they serve are the same no matter what their occupational niche. Here such nonecclesiastical practitioners will find a pastor's view of their common social world.

Deep appreciation is due to the hundreds who have helped me in seeking the community issues and in framing potential approaches to solutions. It is due also to my students in the seminary and, particularly, to those graduate students who have whetted my mind with their abrasive questions and stimulated my learning from their wide reading and discussion. In particular, the Rev. T. W. J. Boadway, in his master's thesis, gave me the suggestion by which this study began. One of the great rewards of teaching on the gradulate level is the education which the inquiring minds of first-rate students bring to their instructors. There is little danger of intellectual stagnation where such students abound. I am much in their debt.

My secretary, Eileen Wilson (Mrs. Peary), patiently converted my original manuscript with its erasures, additions, elisions, and corrections into clear and correct typescript. Further work on the manuscript was done by Peggy Saarima and Beth Hofler (Mrs. Durward). Without their faithful and industrious efforts the present manuscript would have been impossible. I appreciate their carefulness and fidelity, and hope such an investment may have worthy fruition. If this book enables rural pastors to feel more at home in their communities and with themselves, the efforts so many of us have here invested will be amply repaid.

R. C. S.

Contents

1

The Rural Church in a Changing World

Something like a third of all Americans live in rural areas and are in the care of rural pastors. They occupy over ninety percent of our land area and have in their care our nutrition and the bulk of the raw materials out of which technology constructs our modern world. Without them we would be without coal, gas, electricity, meat, bread, gravel, wood, and cement—to name a few of their stewardships. Yet it is relatively easy to overlook them as persons with unique problems.

Today we speak correctly of "urbanization" as a process affecting all our citizens, urban and rural. Then, without being conscious of our logic, we infer that urbanization makes us all the same, wipes out in effect the differences between rural and urban populations.

A more discriminating approach makes clear that the process may have quite distinct effects on people in differing settings. In so far as urbanization benefits us by providing vast resources of personnel and wealth in a limited space, it deprives rather than enriches the rural people it affects. Medical care is an excellent example of this: clinics, hospitals, and staffs make possible superior health care for the generality of urban folk; but low population density denies to rural folk the advantages of modern (urbanized) medicine. Old "Doc" retires or dies and no young doctor is prepared to replace him. Hence the appropriateness of our considering the rural church in changing America.

How many people are involved in the type of community with which we intend to deal? If we apply the adjective "rural" to a community, we are accepting the U.S. Census definition of a rural population division as any such division which has a total population of less than 2,500 inhabitants and is not adjacent to or in contiguous development with a city of 50,000 or more. If our descriptive phrase is "town and country," we are using a church term generally referring to population divisions of less than 10,000. Not all denominations accept this figure, some dropping lower and a few going higher, while occasionally no set figure is given at all. However, the concensus seems to be that town and country churches are churches located and at work in villages or towns of less than 10,000 inhabitants.

Earlier we noted that one third of all Americans were rural: Let us now become more precise. Table I gives the relevant data.

In 1970, 26.5 percent of all Americans were rural. An

TABLE I. UNITED STATES POPULATION

	1970		1960	
	Number	%	Number	%
Total U. S. Population	203,165,573	100.0	179,325,671	100.0
Total Urban Population	149,280,769	73.5	125,283,783	69.9
Urban 2500-9999	14,221,590*	7.0*	13,247,424	7.4
Other Urban	135,059,179*	66.5*	112,036,359	62.5
Total Rural Population	53,884,804	26.5	54,041,888	30.1
Rural Farm	10,361,444*	5.1*	13,444,898	7.5
Rural Nonfarm	43,523,360*	22.2*	40,596,990	22.6
Town and Country Population	68,106,394*	33.5*	67,289,312	37.5

1960—Table 65, U. S. Census of Population, Vol. 1
Charts of Population, Part I. U. S. Summary.
1970—Table 2, U. S. Census of Population Pc (VI)-1,
Final Population Counts.
* Estimates by author

additional 7.0 percent were living in cities of 2,500-9,999. Thus a total of 33.5 percent were town and country persons. From 1960 to 1970 the farm population lost as radically as the rural nonfarm increased, so that the town and country population actually increased between 1960 and 1970 by 1.2 percent.

How may we describe the church which serves town and country people? Of the church in rural areas we can make the following summary statements. It is:

1. *Dominantly Christian.* According to the 1957 U.S. Census report on *Religion Reported by the Civilian Population.*[1] Only one half of one percent of rural nonfarm and one tenth of one percent of rural farm were Jews. 5.1 percent of the rural nonfarm and 4.9

[1] "Religion Reported by the Civilian Population of the United States: March 1957," Current Population Reports Population Characteristics, Series P-20, No. 79. (Feb. 2, 1958).

percent of the rural farm were other religions, no religions, or religions unreported; the remainder called themselves Christian, over 94 percent.

2. *Dominantly Protestant.* Again according to the same study, only 21.2 percent of Roman Catholics were rural, but 43.4 percent of Protestants were rural. Those Protestant were 77.8 percent of rural nonfarm persons and 83.2 percent of farmers.

3. *Characteristically small in numbers.* According to the 1936 census of religious bodies, the average urban church had 541 members against the rural 143. Comparable figures from several denominational groups are Roman Catholic—1,939 and 382; Jewish—1,282 and 239; Congregational churches—340 and 100; Tomlinson Church of God—55 and 35. Generally up-to-date figures are lacking, but in 1965 Methodist churches in communities less than 2,500 averaged 128 members; Methodist churches in communities 2,500–9,999 average 475 members, Methodist churches in communities of 10,000 or more averaged 660 members.

4. *Sharing its pastoral leadership.* Two or more churches are served in a circuit by a single minister, or the minister spends part of his time at another occupation—teaching school or farming, for example.

5. *Reflecting the class and status system of the community.* This the church does in two ways. First, there is a hierarchy of churches within each local community serving various classes and groups and, secondly, the lower in status an individual, the less chance there is that he will belong to or participate in any church.[2]

[2] N. J. Demerath III, *Social Class in American Protestantism* (Chicago: Rand McNally, 1965).
Lloyd W. Warner, Marchia Meeker, Kenneth Eells, eds. *Social Class in America* (Chicago: Science Research Associates, Inc., 1949).

What of changing America? The issue we face is whether we are to think about changes or change. Are the detailed empirical changes that we notice in our culture so many separate trends to which we as churchmen must adjust? Or are the individual and discrete changes specifications under a more fundamental and long-term social movement—a social movement which will color our lives in even more fundamental ways in the generation ahead? Undoubtedly rural churchmen in England in the eighteenth century assembled in order to discuss social changes and how to remedy this or that specific evil. But what those men needed was not an assessment of their individual innovations, but an understanding that their world was shifting from feudalism to modern industrialism. Thus, the question today in America becomes whether we are facing such a similar revolution rather than a series of unrelated social changes.

I am persuaded that we are experiencing, not changes, but symptoms of a fundamental reorientation of our culture. We are living on the accelerating forefront of a revolutionary wave. As the culmination of a long gradual process, there has been, in the Western world, a tremendous increase of mechanical power in the hands of ordinary persons. The increase in mechanical power has made for a reshuffling of our population. Better machinery has enabled fewer and fewer farmers to produce more and more food and fiber on ever enlarging acreages. In 1930 the farm population of the U.S. stood at 29.5 million; by 1970 it had declined to 10.4 million, a loss of 64.7 percent. The index of farm output which stood at 49 in 1946 had risen to 155 by 1965.[3]

Crop production is approximately 80 percent higher per acre than it was at the end of the First World War. The product per breeding animal has almost doubled in the same period. Regularly since 1959 the production per man-hour of American farm labor has shown a 6.6 percent annual increase compared with a 2.6 percent annual increase in nonagricultural affairs. Better seed, fertilizer, and tillage methods, more and more powerful machines have made the difference.[4]

Power increase both in the factory and on the farm has meant an increase in population movement, and the immense increase of power inherent in atomic fission implies an even greater population mobility in the future. Our age is suffering a series of changes because there has been such a multiplication of power in the hands of men that traditional and rational norms of control no longer seem relevant, and man stands alone without significant guidance at the point of his newly achieved power. He does not know how to use his power or how to prevent others from using it to destroy him. He no longer knows what his duty is or where his safety lies.

At the same time that man has gained this power, which now seems to threaten him, his mobility has separated him from his fellows. In 1961 only 79.4 percent of our population a year old and above was

[3] *Food & Fiber for the Future* (Washington, D.C.: U.S. Government Printing Office, July, 1967), p. 152.
[4] *Background on U.S. Agriculture* (Leaflet No. 491, U.S. Department of Agriculture [rev. March, 1966]).

living in the same house as in 1960, while 13.7 percent were living in a different house in the same county and 6.3 percent were living in a different county. Of the remainder, .6 percent had been out of the country in 1960.[5] Figures for 1967 show the trends are consistent throughout the decade: those listed were 11.6 percent having moved in the previous year within the same county and 6.7 percent having moved to another county.[6] The stability and the personal standards that come from living in a physically familiar setting and being in daily contact with people who have known us and our fathers before us are gone, not only for most urban people but for many rural people as well. The characteristic human reaction is a feeling of strangeness, loneliness, and isolation in the face of new and unfamiliar neighbors and responsibilities.

The members of an adult Sunday school class in a Chicago suburb were asked to look around them and then write the names of as many members of the class as they could. The class had already had ten sessions in its current series. Eighty-three persons were in attendance and all eighty-three turned in lists of names. The average number named per list was 22 persons. Ten of those present were not members of the church, and they listed on the average only 7 names; the 73 church members averaged 24 names on their lists. Men averaged 19 and women 23. The highest number named by any person was 58 and only six of the group were able

[5] Table 34, *Statistical Abstract of the United States* (Washington, D.C.: U.S. Dept. of Commerce, 1962), p. 38.
[6] Table 37, *Statistical Abstract of the United States* (Washington, D.C.: U.S. Dept. of Commerce, 1968), p. 38.

to name 40 or more persons, approximately half those present. The loneliness of our day cannot better be illustrated than by the fact that, in a church school class which had met for ten weeks and in which the overwhelming majority were members of the same local church, the average member was able to name only 25 percent of those who were his fellow students in the class.

In the process of the expansion of power and the diffusion of persons, rural society is a part of our total society. If ever rural could be detached from general society, it certainly cannot be now. Streams of urban refugees are constantly invading rural areas, particularly in the fringes. Rural refugees are just as constantly and in greater numbers invading both the central city and the fringe itself. This invasion of city and country alike by strangers means that, as we Americans have grown more powerful, we have become more estranged from one another and hence we feel increasingly isolated and alone.

Now, to be at once powerful and lonely makes a man subject to three fears. First, he fears the strangers that are all around him. Daily he finds himself related to persons whom he does not understand and trust. Then he fears what he will do to these strangers with the new power he has. Having no cue as to how he should treat them, he distrusts and fears his own ability to control this new power. And last, through the psychological mechanism of projection, he fears what these powerful strangers will do to him.

People who are afraid of their powers, their neighbors, and themselves, run away. The social changes of our day may be understood as so many different flights from these fears. There is, first of all, the flight to the family. In the period immediately following the end of hostilities in the Second World War, there was a sharp rise in the marriage rate and an unexpected rise in the birthrate—a rise that maintained itself over a series of years. It seems likely that this rise represents not just the normal postwar marriage and birth increase, but the flight of millions of couples into domestic life in the hope that, in the familiar pattern of family and parenthood, there would come a surcease from the intolerable loneliness of the war and its aftermath. But the family exists, not as an asylum from responsibility and fear, but as a cooperative enterprise demanding mature participation. The mounting divorce rates and the vandalism of children and youth show how fragile the family is as a refuge in our flight from fear.

Another related flight is the flight to informality—the cult of the sport shirt, slacks and jeans. The outpouring of undressed and half-dressed humanity, characteristic of restaurant and hotel life in our day, and seen in the shopping crowds of the great city or the market town suggests that people are desperately seeking to recover a sense of familiarity with their neighbors. This informal attire is the badge, the wistful symbol of their passion to be considered common folks among other folks. But when informality becomes a fad it ends up, not as informality, but as a highly stylized fashion of its own. And so a teenager changes undershirts three times before he gets just the proper "V" effect at the throat of his open sport shirt. The cult of the informal becomes the champion and enforcer of a new formalism. We do not find in it a real relief from our loneliness.

A second major flight is the flight to delusion. This flight motivates the witch hunts for domestic Communists and fellow travelers and the guilt-by-association school of public opinion. Unhappy, insecure people are always looking for a scapegoat, a definite person or group against which they can discharge the animosity and fears aroused within them. They are ready to give authority and prestige to the leader who realizes their psychological tensions and helps them to discharge their fears in the assurance that the Communist rascals are being found out and expelled from their seats of leadership and power. Millions of Americans have fled from their fears by displacing them upon Communists and liberals found guilty by association; but there is no assurance that such purchased freedom from fear will long endure. Indeed, there is every reason to believe that, since what we fear is our power and our loneliness, and only by projection the Communists, our fears will return to us with Monday morning's hangover, and we shall be obliged to resort to renewed and greater excesses to still our inner pangs. Many of us who see so clearly the danger of this flight to delusion are tempted to it ourselves in identifying the evil with such of its practitioners as McCarthy or Jenner or Velde. These men are not the evil itself but simply opportunists riding on our people's fears. Let us keep in focus what the real issue is:

the expansion of our powers—the diffusion of our people. When we remember this, we can understand how it seems easier to deal with atomic power in Russian hands than to discipline our own hands in their use of such power, particularly when an unrecognized but pervasive sense of guilt for the civilian dead of Hiroshima and Nagasaki is among us.

A third flight is the flight to authoritarianism. When things are uncertain, it is always easier to be ordered around than to order ourselves. The increasing idealization and acceptance of military men in public life are indications of this trend. The continuance of the draft and the renewed appeal for universal military training are signs that our fellows, intolerably burdened by the power available to them and bereft of the support of a warm group life, are accepting the regimentation of our common life and the loss of our basic freedoms as the price of some small sense of security. But dependence breeds dependence, and we shall grow personally weaker the more we turn to the politically, militarily, economically, or ecclesiastically mighty for direction and help.

There is one sense in which the church must bear special responsibility for the flights of our day. In earlier generations religion provided a proper object against which popular fears could be displaced. In its vivid preaching of hell, damnation, the devil, and the eternal punishment of the wicked, it gave a socially sanctioned basis for the displacement of fear. It is certainly more healthy from the point of view of social order for a man to displace his fears on eternal punishment than to displace them on Communists. The church, in taking away from men any vivid sense of future punishment, has taken away one possibility of fear displacement. I do not think that the churches should return to their old preachments, but we must be aware of what society lost when we took hell away. And we must woo and win our people away from the new displacements as effectively as we did from the old hell.

The pages which follow will outline a response which town and country churches and their pastors may make to the changes of our day. This response grows out of the faith that social change is amenable to understanding and control. We are only pawns of change when we refuse to learn and use the perspectives and skills which social science has given us. A detailing of that perspective and the related skills it offers is the task we now confront.

2

Is Knowledge Power?

"Action," "activist," and "militant" are popular words among churchmen today in reaction to such changes as we have mentioned in the preceding discussion; young pastors in particular want to be "where the action is." "Involvement" for themselves and their congregations is the norm by which they increasingly determine fidelity to their vocation. It is also the norm by which they appraise curricula, teachers, and learning in professional training for ministry.

The result of this drive—unintended but ruthless nonetheless—is ahistoricism and anti-intellectualism. A narrow concentration on present problems tends to make contemporary and personal empiricism the rule of faith and knowledge. Knowledge for the sake of the simple satisfaction of human curiosity is condemned as an effete luxury we cannot afford. Knowledge as a basis for action is regarded as unnecessary, indeed suspect, as a device for postponing the radical actions we ought to take. "We know what we ought to do," we are told, "what we need is the courage to do it."

What evidence supports this skeptical conclusion regarding formal knowledge? Many years ago Thorstein Veblen[1] discussed the nonadjustive character of some education under the term, "trained incapacity." In any complex organization, he pointed out, the better trained a man is for his particular job, the less equipped he is to understand other positions and responsibilities in the division of labor, and the less likely he is to be aware when change is needed in the management of his particular task. His very expertness makes him inflexible, confident that he knows the answer to any problem, unable to see totalities because he is so close to his particularity. His knowledge, far from giving him power, makes him rigid and unadjustive in any situation of crisis or change.

But is what Veblen says of the bureaucrat true of the pastor? Are we victims of "trained incapacity"? Specialists, educated professionals, indeed we are, and subject to the risk that such training carries, prone to define our situation and its problems in the light of the training we have received. The better we have digested that training, the more we feel confident in situations which we may entirely misread. T. W. J. Boadway sought to test the applicability of the Veblen thesis to

[1] Robert Dubin, *The World of Work* (Englewood Cliffs, N. J.: Prentice-Hall, 1958).

town and country Baptist pastors in one region of
Canada.[2] A review of his findings will help us understand the nature of "training incapacity" as it affects
the ministry.

We begin with the fact that the Baptists in Ontario
have a high standard of ministerial preparation. The
norm is that a pastor should be both a university and
seminary graduate. However, in common with other
denominations, the Baptists face a scarcity of ministers, which bears down with particular weight upon
town and country churches. Hence men who have less
than the required amount of training must be used as
pastors. The pastors studied by Boadway ranged in
education from men with training limited to Bible
school and correspondence courses to men who had
completed college and seminary and had taken advanced post-seminary work. Those with college and
seminary training had come through an academically
first-rate classical education. They were skilled in biblical languages and textual exegesis, church history,
and systematic theology. But they had had little or no
social science. As a control group, Boadway studied a
group of Methodist pastors in northern Wisconsin,
men serving in situations ecologically and demograph-
ically much like that of the Ontario pastors. They dif-
fered, however, in the fact that those who had full
preparation, college and seminary degrees, had completed their work in institutions in which social science

[2] "Social Sensitivity in the Baptist Town and Country Ministry of the Georgian Bay and Owen Sound Associations of
Ontario, Canada" (Evanston, Illinois: 1963).

had a respectable, if not a prominent, place in the curriculum.

The thesis he sought to evaluate was that Baptist town and country pastors, because of their specialized training, would be less sensitive to community forces and conditions the more nearly they conformed to the standard of education their church required. Their training, he reasoned, would predispose them to define their situations and responsibilities in biblical and theological terms unrelated to the social setting of their parishioners. To test their knowledge of their communities he developed a simple questionnaire which was administered in an informal interview with each pastor. From each pastor's response to the questions Boadway was able to give him a rating on social sensitivity.

Boadway found that among Baptist pastors in northern Ontario there was a rank correlation of minus .31 between educational attainment and social awareness in the local community. Among the Methodist pastors in northeastern Wisconsin, his control group, there was no correlation whatever between education and social awareness. The numbers are too small and the areas too limited to justify general conclusions on the basis of these facts, but the conclusions generate strong plausibility for a general application of the hypothesis. Boadway himself summarizes his study thus:

. . . the findings of this exploratory study strongly indicate that the absence of sociologically oriented teachings at the seminary level of ministerial education produces within the ministers . . . a trained incapacity to observe the social phenomena of their communities, and thus, an inability to relate . . . the church as a subsystem of society to the other subsystems of community life.[3]

The indications of Boadway's study are that a purely classical training may make a minister insensitive to social realities about him, but it also carries the possible implication that an education in which social studies have a part may have no positive effect on sensitizing the minister, though it may not leave him insensitive. Knowledge would seem to have a negative or inhibiting power but no demonstrated positive power.

To continue the exploration of the role of knowledge in the town and country pastor's work, a group of graduate students under the direction of the author developed a more involved and comprehensive study.[4] They took counsel of the members of the Rural Sociological Society to determine what sociological concepts those scholars thought most important for the practicing rural pastor to understand. A list of ten concepts emerged from the responses of 204 sociologists, concepts which a majority regarded as "of major importance." An objective test to determine whether a pastor understood the several concepts in a sociological perspective was devised and given to 330 Methodist town and country pastors chosen at random across the U.S.A. It then became possible to relate the score a pastor made on this test to his educational background

[3] *Ibid.*
[4] Rockwell C. Smith, Clifford M. Black, Stephen G. Cobb, S. Burkett Milner, *The Role of Rural Social Science in Theological Education* (Evanston, Ill.: Bureau of Social and Religious Research, Garrett, 1969).

on the one hand and to the program in his church and its community on the other, and thus to determine, as Boadway had not been able to do, the positive relationship of sociological sophistication on the pastor's part and the community outreach by the churches he serves.

The reader interested in the details of the study may consult the report. Here we wish only to list its conclusions in summary form.

1. Ministers who have had college and seminary courses in sociology tend to react in sociological terms of the test more frequently than ministers without such training.
2. Ministers who have read books in the field likewise react more sociologically on the test than do unread ministers.
3. Ministers who rate high sociologically on the test serve churches which show a higher service concern for their communities than other churches.
4. There is no demonstrated relationship overall between high sociological scores and efficiency in church maintenance.
5. There is a positive relationship between high scores on the test and member recruitment and per capita giving in churches served by high-scoring pastors.

A few statistics will indicate the relationships specifically which we have stated in summary form. Among the 19 ministers whose sociological test scores were less than three (on a ten-point scale), the average community outreach index for churches served was 4.2.

Among churches served by the 22 ministers scoring 9 or 10 on the test, the average community outreach score was 10.6. The low-scoring ministers served churches with an ecclesiastical efficiency index averaging 21.8, while those with the high scores served churches with an ecclesiastical index average of 23.2. The startling difference in the community outreach scores is not reflected in church maintenance scores. A similar pattern is reflected in the entire sample as well as in the extremes: though there is a real positive correlation between scores and community outreach throughout the whole range of the distribution, there is no demonstrable correlation between scores and ecclesiastical effectiveness.

Back to our original question in this chapter: Is knowledge power? We conclude that the knowledge classically assumed to be essential for the training of a pastor may be a handicap to him in the community affairs of his parish by giving him a sense of confidence and expertness unrelated to the everyday life of his people. On the other hand, social science knowledge enables a pastor to lead his people to involvement in their communities. It does not, however, add to his capacity to manage the administrative affairs of the church expertly.

These conclusions grow out of the empirical evidence; the further question inevitably arises as to how social science knowledge helps or fails to help the pastor himself in his work. Here we can only speculate, or develop additional hypotheses for later research. It appears, first, that sociological sophistication makes a man aware of the social processes at work in his community. He notes social structures and developments which the untutored person misses: selective population mobility, shifting age structure, the rise of a commuter category of citizens with economic interests outside the local community, neighborhood decline, the local class structure and its ramifications of privilege, communication patterns, and power struggles. As a minister, he is constantly called to help persons whose lives are affected by these social facts. He will be a more effective helper if he is not blind to the social environment in which his parishioners struggle.

Second, as a consequence of this awareness he will feel at home in the community. What goes on will make sense to him even when he is unhappy about it. He will not feel menaced by some unmanageable threat, but he will see himself confronting assessable and manageable social forces. His natural tendency to condemnation will be tempered by intelligent appraisal of trends and opportunities for leadership in the community. Ordering and forbidding will give way to understanding and guiding because the pastor will feel confident of his place in the community and of his ability to manage its forces.

And this empowering of the pastor is the third potential contribution of social science: it teaches him how change takes place in groups and how he can bring change about. Such knowledge of the course of change is power of a high order. But our data suggest that while pastors use this knowledge—when they have it—in the community in which they work, they less frequently and less effectively use it in their churches. Apparently pastors fail to see that the church is a group among groups and that the forces that work in the Grange or the Farm Bureau work in the church as well. Perhaps the church is too close to us, means too much, for us to see its human side. We do not denigrate the glory of the church when we understand it in terms of social dynamics. God did not make the church group different from other groups; he is the Creator of all. Social science knowledge has the power not only to make a more relevant church but also to make a more efficient one.

With this conviction of the relevance and power of sociological know-how to the pastor's task we move ahead. We plan to attempt some understanding of the overall perspective in which sociologists work, and then to develop in detail the meaning of those concepts regarded by rural sociologists as contributing essential knowledge to the effective work of the town and country pastor. We continue this intellectual analysis in the conviction that such knowledge is power indeed.

3

The Sociological Perspective

The sociologist lives and learns in the world we all live in; nothing is unique about his world except his perception of it. The concepts with which he works, the processes which he analyzes, the regularities which he describes take their unity from the perspective with which he begins, the standpoint from which he surveys our common world. Our study of sociological concepts will be meaningful only if we first understand the perspective from which the sociologist makes his observations.

To begin with, the sociologist is a student rather than an actor; his goal is to understand society, not to evaluate or revolutionize it, so that an element of detachment (sometimes interpreted as indifference) characterizes his attitudes. His is the stance of the spectator rather than of the participant; he attempts with all the skills of his craft to note the forces, obvious and subtle, which are at work in whatever social situation he observes; he does not attempt *as sociologist* to control the forces or change the direction of their movement.

The italicized words "as sociologist" are most important here. They stress the fact that a sociologist like any and every other worker is a great deal more than his job. He is, in fact, a husband, a father, an American, a black, a Methodist, a Democrat, an Air Force reservist, etc. etc. These several positions in society carry with them commitments and loyalties which the sociologist as a man and citizen has responsibilities to recognize. In these positions he does participate in the social life and not just observe it. But when he works and writes as a sociologist, a part of his craft is to maintain a mind as free from bias as possible. His sociological conviction is that conclusions reflecting not his personal predilections but objective observation will alone serve his particular interests as well as the public interest in either the long or the short run.

This sociological conviction is itself an article of faith, of course, a faith that is an element in Western democracy. Other cultures regard social investigation as the application of official social perspectives to the group life studied by the scholar. There his function as investigator is to show how current social developments reflect the official ideology. And pressure to reflect "the American point of view" is not unfelt by the American sociologist. Nonetheless his settled conviction is that his responsibility is not to offer rationalization for the social status quo, but rather to enable citizens to understand the total functioning of the society of which they are a part. He resists any attempt to bring his conclusions in line with preconceived social policy, because he is convinced that such resistance alone will make his conclusions socially useful.

A certain intellectual imperialism has been suggested by our discussion thus far; we hasten to state explicitly that sociology is only one of a number of social sciences. It is not the only academic discipline which studies society. Similar social disciplines are economics, anthropology, political science, social history. What distinguishes the sociologist from other students of social life is his focus not on a specialized form of association (economics dealing with wealth-getting and wealth distribution, for example) but on human association as such. Wherever men are in relationship to other men for whatever reason, or for no apparent reason, the sociologist is concerned to study their relationship.

The sociologist, then, is a student of society, an objective student of society seeking to understand it without reference to his own biases or preferences, a student who focuses on human association of every kind and reports what he finds. This is not to suggest that the sociologist ignores the values people hold; he insists that he cannot understand their acts unless he knows what they think the acts will produce, what meaning the acts have for them. He only refuses to establish a hierarchy of meanings or to say that one meaning is better, truer, or richer than another. He leaves this adjudication to the ethicist, the philosopher, and the religionist.

To say one wants to understand society and its processes is to imply that society has an order which can be discovered, that amidst the rich variegation of observed groups is an ordered correlation of significant variables from group to group in the social process. This assumption underlies the work of any scientist. We believe that there are regularities in social relationships which can be ascertained, and that a knowledge of these permits us to predict with accuracy the outcome of given courses of action in society.

Does such an assumption lead to the conclusion that human freedom is illusory and planned social change impossible? So to conclude is to confound order with determinism. Such human freedom as underlies social planning is simply the capacity to anticipate the future result of present action and thus to make the future a determiner in the present. But only if there is a dependable calculus of the relationship of present and future conditions is there any possibility of freedom. Social freedom is only possible through a knowledge of the dependable courses of social processes. The more social determinism sociology reveals, the more potential freedom we possess.

Out of this standpoint there arise three insights that are commonly accepted and that have become the base from which the sociologist works. The first is the conviction that man's most intimate and natural environment is society: there is no such thing as a non-group man. Human survival and the development of what we understand to be elementary human nature de-

pends upon the existence of a human organism in and
its interaction with others in a group. To modern man
the physical and technological works seem to be most
real, just as to medieval man the supernatural world
seemed most real; but each man is simply reflecting
the stance of his culture, what his interrelationships
with other men and women have taught him to feel
and to take as axiomatic. It is from his prior experience of men that he derives all his other certainties.
As a French sociologist put it: "The first categories
of things are categories of persons."

Social interaction, then, is the basic process by which
human organisms become human beings, the behavior
out of which human nature emerges and comes to self-
expression. One of the concepts to which we shall give
detailed analysis in a later chapter is the concept of
"interaction." Here we wish only to stress the fact that
sociologists are constantly taking the concept of social
interaction for granted as fundamental to any understanding of man. Sociologists do not argue as to
whether man is a social animal or not; they assume it.

A second primary insight is that most social interaction takes place through symbols; man relates himself to his fellows through the use of conventionally
agreed upon signs which stand for things, attitudes,
acts, and regulations. The red-orange-green sequence
of traffic control lights is an example of the control of
human relationships that inheres in purely arbitrary
symbols. The wave of the hand, the outstretched hand
of greeting, the clenched fist of threat, the "V" for
victory or for peace gestures are familiar manual symbols, the meaning of which seems unmistakable though

such meanings are essentially conventional to Western culture.

The great common fund of symbols, however, is in language; through the conventions of speech we are able to reach out and relate to persons in infinitely subtle ways. And precisely because of this infinite richness of meaning, language becomes a real barrier between persons if they happen to be schooled in different languages. If you have tried to communicate with a person who does not speak English while you do, you have experienced the real sense of frustration that arises in the relationship—there is so much you want to say to one another and so little that you can.

It is fashionable to say "one picture is worth a thousand words." And all of us know what graphic emotional impact a picture can have. But pictures, whether in newsprint or on television, are ambiguous at best. They allow us a freedom to offer our own interpretations of the meaning of what is happening. Language still is the most precise vehicle we have for interrelating to one another. Granted that it can be used to hinder communication, to hide men's meanings— nonetheless it is, when honestly used, our most comprehensive and significant symbol system. We note, however, that there is still much subjectivity in our use of words and our response to them. The tone in which a word is uttered may communicate more than the word itself.

A third insight which sociologists generally accept is that all social relationships serve a function for the persons whose relationships they are and for the total society of which those persons are a part. The theoretical school which stresses this insight is referred to as "functionalism," but all sociologists are functionalist in their outlook, whether or not they accept the term as applying to their research. They are convinced that every social arrangement subserves some significant function for its society, and that a part of their responsibility is to find out what that function, or more properly, those functions are.

Robert K. Merton has distinguished between manifest and latent functions.[1] Manifest functions are obvious, the stated functions of relationships and institutions. Prostitution obviously functions to reduce the sexual tensions of single males or males not otherwise adequately satisfied sexually. Its function in tension management is clear. But it may also function as a means of employment and support for a surplus female population and as a means of controlling what might otherwise become a disastrously high birthrate with consequent overpopulation. These latter functions are latent. Failure to understand latent functions of social institutions like prostitution has involved well-meaning persons in ineffective methods for controlling them.

Sometimes this social insight is interpreted by critics as guaranteeing that sociologists will be conservative in their social impact—that they will, in fact, justify almost any social evil because they can point to real and important functions that it serves. Sociologists answer that such is not the case at all; that, indeed, well-meaning reformers who do not take into account the real functions served by socially evil rela-

[1] *Social Theory and Social Structure* (New York: The Free Press, 1949), chapter 1.

tionships are never likely to change those relationships. An accurate knowledge of social dynamics must precede any effective social change.

The sociologist has a special methodological handicap because his subject matter is shared on the level of intimate acquaintance with all of us. Every man knows society, it is a kind of second skin in which he constantly lives. If the sociologist is to push beyond common sense to some sophisticated understanding of society, he must develop special methods of observation.

Statistical expression of social facts and their elaboration by mathematical techniques (infinitely expanded by computer technology in our day) is one of his first attempts at precise observation not possible in everyday social experience. But statistical manipulation involves many problems: what is the unit we shall count, by what unit shall we measure, or is the order of items all we are interested in? Some social data involves simply classification: for example, census data on country-of-origin of citizens, England, France, etc. We can give the total number in each category, but the categories bear no mathematically defined relationship to one another. Such statistical distributions are referred to as nominal.

Sometimes the data so classified are susceptible to ordering, and we can place items in a table so that they exceed one another as we progress through the table. Studies of social class or of prestige depend upon an ordering of persons in such a way that persons in the upper class are clearly "superior" to all other persons in other classes and persons in the middle class are "superior" to lower class persons but "inferior" to upper class. Here our categories do bear a mathematically ordered relationship to one another.

Finally, it is occasionally possible to develop social data in which there are independently existing and numerable units. We then are dealing with cardinal numbers. A population distribution in which age is the factor would be such a case. In the present state of the science, however, most sociological data are not amenable to expression in cardinal numbers.

The difficulty which faces the sociologist is that once any collection of data is given numerical expression it can be subjected to any and all mathematical manipulations. But only cardinal numbers are properly the subject of the whole scale of mathematical usage. The temptation is to put our data into the computer and to come out with a series of tables and measurements which look impressive but are not justified by the original data from which they are calculated. The sophisticated sociologist must be as alert to what measurements he cannot apply to his data as to what he will apply.

And the difficulty which we outline here occurs again and again with other methods he uses. The interview is one such puzzling method. When we talk to another person to elicit his opinions or sentiments, how much of him do we get and how much of ourselves do we project to him and receive back from him? When we deal with the concept of "communication," we shall return to this question. Here we only point to the issue as a methodological problem of the sociological perspective.

What we have said in this chapter will lead the pastor to understand something of the perspective within which and the limitations under which the sociologist works. Looking at our common life as a fellow human, the sociologist must yet devise ways and means for undercutting the common prejudice or assumption and reaching through to the functioning reality. As he succeeds he helps us all to be more effectively human within the communities where we live, work, and lead.

4

Norms and Values

Most pastors would regard themselves as specialists in the field of human values; we are always ready to talk in terms of ultimate truth and goodness. And our penchant for concern with these matters is supported by the judgment of rural sociologists who, when asked to rate some fifty sociological concepts in terms of their relative importance to a minister at work in town and country, put "norms and values" ahead of all the others. Over three fourths of these social scientists rated the concept of "norms and values" as "of major importance" to the rural pastor. Beginning then on this common ground, let us explore the terms to see what sociologists have to add to our understanding of them.

A value is anything to which men attach a preference. Values grow out of, and are related to, needs of the human individual, but they are not to be understood entirely in terms of need, for at every point man elaborates the satisfaction of his basic needs in manifold ways. Indeed we might well say that a value is a socially conditioned statement of a need satisfaction. Pastors by training think of values as given by God: the truth is revealed to man in the Bible, for example; or goodness is defined by the Ten Commandments given by God to Moses. Sociologists would not necessarily reject such an approach, but they would understand the divine definition of values as mediated through social channels; the Bible, they would insist, is the church's book growing out of insights revealed to men in and through the Christian fellowship. They would go on to stress that values have their objectivity in the fact that they root in the limitations and possibilities inherent in the order of nature, or in the created order, to use a religious term.

What needs underlie the social scaffolding of value? First are the basic subsistence needs: air, water, food, shelter. To survive, the human organism must have ready and constant access to these satisfactions. But this scaffolding of organic needs is quickly covered with social elaborations, so that the values which relate to their satisfaction are socially defined. A man can survive on a handful of berries and raw fish, but none of us would regard that as an adequate meal. The whole elaborate ritual of table cloth, napkins, gleaming silverware, fine china, and food elaborately prepared and served with evident concern for beauty and variety is an indication of what man does in elaborating values from his basic needs. Indeed, so far has this social elaboration gone that a religious man does not regard his meal as properly begun until he has offered a prayer of thanks to God over it.

Less obvious but not less real and pressing is our need for emotional response, for interpersonal warmth and attention. We know that an infant whose mother has rejected him will reject nourishment and actually die of starvation because of his need for the emotional warmth his mother once supplied. Pediatric wards in hospitals employ women to do nothing but provide surrogate emotional mothering to rejected infants; their work is simply to hold, rock, talk, or sing to the baby and generally to provide an environment of personal affection. Unless the child feels this emotional response, he may well fail to survive no matter how adequate the physical care provided for him.

A third basic need involves our desire to have a known and dependable position in relationship to our fellows; we say that we want to know who we are and where we stand with those around us. The opinion of our fellows is important to us. We require an inner sense of dignity growing out of our prior sense of their approval. We speak of a new automobile or a new house as a "status symbol," indicating that a car or a home does something more than meet our physical needs; they help to locate us in the community of esteem of people around us. The Negro asserting "black is beautiful" is accepting his blackness rather than seeking to escape it, and is telling his society that he expects to be recognized and approved for what he is.

The minister who wears a clerical collar is using another device to identify himself and to establish his privileged position with those around him.

A fourth need is evident in our experience of boredom and in our demand for excitement and change. Life's routine, no matter how adequate, is never enough; we seek adventure. The absorption of men and women around the world in the moon walks of our astronauts is one indication of our deep need for novelty. Fad, fashion, the bizarre, and the occult are all reflections of our inner passion to be different, to do the novel, to live dangerously. Bread—life's securities —is important, but "man does not live by bread alone." The mountain climber, the wilderness traveler, the drag racer, the free thinker are all seeking to satisfy the need for adventure and discovery.

W. I. Thomas summarized this analysis of needs in his listing of the four wishes which he held govern human motivation and set the life style of the individual person as one or another of the wishes dominates his behavior.[1] He referred to the wish for security, the wish for new experience, the wish for recognition, and the wish for response. All these wishes reflect basic and perennial needs of persons. From these needs we elaborate the values that our society seeks to safeguard and to increase.

In passing we observe that these four areas of need do not present a coherent unity. Satisfaction of one set of needs may involve the denial of others. The student seeking new truth may impoverish himself in order to carry on his studies. New experience is more important

[1] *The Unadjusted Girl* (Boston: Little, Brown, 1923).

to him than security. A young woman may deprive herself of food if she is convinced that the resultant slimming of her body will make her more attractive to young men. Response asserts itself against security. A minister may neglect his family in order to achieve superior placement in the ministry; desire for recognition has, in his case, triumphed over the need for emotional response. Another minister may soft-pedal the innovative thrust of his preaching in order to keep in the good graces of conservative laymen and thus preserve his livelihood; here security needs have taken first place to the need for new experience. There is a certain built-in conflict among the needs of life so that, sooner or later, persons and societies have to choose among the ends for which they will expend their strictly limited resources.

Norms are prescriptions for proper behavior which are intended to secure and maintain the values men seek. A general value must be converted to a practical prescription and standard if we are to realize it together in society. Norms always grow out of human association. We operate in terms of norms so constantly that we are unaware of their existence until we pause to consider our behavior. An American norm is that drivers proceed on the right. An intensely motorized generation like ours comes to behave almost as if this norm were written into our physical structure, yet we know that driving to the right is only a convention and that other countries even more industrial than ours—England is a case in point—drive to the left. The security of life of our people depends upon the constancy with which we keep to the right, yet keeping to the right is not an eternal principle or objective prescription; it is simply a societal norm which guarantees to us, in so far as a guarantee is possible, safety on the highway. To drive to the left would be equally effective, but what is peremptory is that everyone should drive in the same terms. Driving to the right is one of the norms of our culture by which we achieve the value of security.

The illustration we have used involves a norm that is established in the formal law of the country and is enforced by legal standards. Not all, indeed not most, norms have this formal legal statement and support; for instance, another norm in our culture is that gentlemen rise when a lady enters the room and remain standing until she is seated. There is no law that states this as a requirement obligatory upon the male populace, but not to behave in this fashion is to risk the application of informal sanctions—these may be as simple as not being invited to the homes of our acquaintances because of our careless manners, and they may involve penalties as harsh as ridicule and social ostracism.

Norms are always the products of social interaction, but we can distinguish five levels of norm formation. First there are the most general norms, which are the product of our total society. Driving to the right is one such norm; not smoking on the bus or subway is another; coming to work on time is a third, and the list might be endlessly expanded. These norms prescribe the appropriate behavior for an American human: of many such norms we are not even aware because our personhood is so intimately bound up in them. Only when we visit a quite different culture do we become aware of our own distinctive norms.

A second level of norm formation is that of the social class. Ours is a society of strata among which standards differ. That the family should eat at least the evening meal as a unit is a norm for middle class society; but among lower class persons, family members eat when they choose and as they can. The pastor who stresses the importance of grace at meals may find a ready hearing among his middle class parishioners, yet be met by total lack of comprehension where lower class members are concerned. If a family never eats together or does so only on rare and accidental occasions, family prayer at meat is without practical meaning.

Regional societies within American society have their own peculiar and characteristic norms. A rural Vermonter transported to rural New Mexico will find himself sensitive to a whole set of expectations that he never felt before. The plentiful water that he knew at home accustomed him to a perspective which he must now rapidly shift in an area of limited moisture. His norms of housing, reflecting the cold and snow of Vermont, will shift as he encounters the sun and dryness of the southwest. His Anglo-Saxon norms will encounter and be confused by the Indian and Spanish norms of his new home. Regional societies are norm-building agents.

A characteristic development of modern technological and industrial society is the large-scale organization. More and more of us find ourselves living in an environment which some organization constructs for us. Methodist pastors have always been itinerants moving at the behest of ecclesiastical superiors. Their wives and children became adept at packing and moving to a new charge, entering new school systems, establishing new circles of friendship. But they were always conscious of the ephemeral nature of these relationships; their abiding loyalty and center of reference was the annual conference and the fellowship of the ministry. What was once unique to the Methodist itinerancy has now become increasingly the mark of millions of Americans. They belong to one of the major corporations: they are Swift people or General Motors or Westinghouse or IBM. They shuttle around the nation and indeed around the world as representatives of their respective organizations. They are, to use Whyte's expressive phrase, "organization men." [2] Their norms are laid down for them by their membership in the organization, so that whatever their immediate locale and setting, their constant and ultimate reference is the organization and what they have come to believe it expects of them.

Finally, norms grow out of the immediate group life in which we are participants. A local Baptist church will share certain norms with all Baptists, the organizational norms, but it will also have particular and peculiar norms of its own. The seating pattern in the sanctuary at Sunday morning worship is one such unique and local norm. The hour of church service, the pattern of worship, and the behavior when the

[2] William Hollingsworth Whyte, *The Organization Man* (New York: Simon and Schuster, 1956).

service is over are other familiar expressions of local church norms.

Families are groups with their special norms involving, among others, such diverse matters as the order of the use of the bathroom on weekday mornings, the reception and entertainment of guests, family recreation, TV viewing, and the tasks to be performed by the several members of the household. Children who for the first time visit a home with different norms are startled to find people behaving in a way which, to them, seems slightly abnormal and inhuman, so familiar are they with the norms set and practiced by their own family.

All of us, of course, participate in norm-creating associations on all five levels; thus the stage is set for conflict among the norms, with related conflict of values. Societal norms and regional norms may frequently be in conflict, as witness the struggle now going on in America over school integration. There is even no guarantee that the norms formed at any single level will be in harmony. Americans state their belief in law and order on the one hand but tolerate and, on occasion, encourage a degree of lawlessness on the part of law-enforcing agencies themselves in dealing with suspected criminals. Again and again the working pastor has noted the tension between the norms of the national denomination of which he is a minister (organizational norms) and the norms of the local church (immediate group) which he serves as minister.

The sociologist teaches us that the values and norms with which we work from day to day as churchmen are defined by and have their dynamic in the group life of which the church is a part. Whenever we have norms which conflict, we have the projection of groups in conflict; that is why rational argument is so often powerless in resolving a conflict of norms in the local community. What is threatened by any accommodation of norms is not only the values themselves, but the prestige and authority of the groups involved. To give up one norm for another or even to make any substantial adjustment of a norm will seem to the group members involved to be disloyalty to the group itself, indeed a threat to the group's continued existence. In changing values and transforming norms we are altering the structure and authority of the groups to which our people belong. Such alteration is no mere intellectual task, the subject of rational debate and intelligent decision; any effective alteration of norms involves a knowledge of the societal and group structure of a community and a sophisticated operation within that structure.

5

The Community

Most pastors would agree with rural sociologists that the concept of the community is an important one to understand if the pastor is to serve his church significantly. But when we use the term "community" with reference to our local situation, we are confronted with misunderstandings and ambiguities. It will help us then to determine what it is the sociologist is talking about when he uses the term, how he suggests we determine the limits of the local community, how he interprets what has been happening historically to American town and country communities, what he sees as likely to happen to them in the future for which we churchmen are required to plan.

As sociologists use the term "community," it refers first of all to people, as distinct from the animal or plant communities which are the subject matter of the ecologist. We are dealing with communities of men and women. Such a statement is important to our understanding because, when we get to talking about the boundaries of a community and the services available therein, we are in danger of reifying such structural items as if they made the community. We repeat that the community is always people in relationship to one another, doing things together including, on occasion, fighting one another. If there are no people, there is no community. A town and country community is, first of all, people.

A community is the primary living space of its members; within its boundaries they must find the basic services which are needed to meet their individual and collective needs. There must be agencies of transportation and communication, trade and finance, education, professional service, and social and religious service. Thus a complex interrelationship between geographic area and services offered develops. In the early nineteen-hundreds Warren Wilson described American town and country communities in terms of the "team haul." Around a small town containing various service establishments, the countryside to the limit of round-trip distance a team of horses could cover in a day constituted the characteristic rural community. Obviously technology changes this pattern, and in two directions. First of all, new means of transportation and communication make possible a greater distance of outreach in service. In addition, technological efficiency on the farm and the consequent decline in rural population make it necessary that economic and social institutions and agencies extend their areas of service if they are to survive. General technology, both on and off the farm, has developed in a pattern requiring constant extension of community boundaries.

A community is also a matter of feeling; unless people feel that they belong to one another in a distinctive and characteristic way, they do not possess a community. Persons in relationship with other persons never interrelate without developing emotional attachments and animosities. Farm people and villagers unite in speaking of their community as "our town." And here is a source of one of the tensions that rural leaders are called on to manage: technology may make a particular small rural service center obsolete, yet the loyalties which have bound its farm hinterland to it do not change at the same pace; economic rationalization and social sentiment are in head-on conflict.

To summarize, a community refers to (1) people within a (2) specifically delimited geographic setting, dependent upon a (3) common center for social and economic services, and sharing (4) common emotional attachments and loyalties. In dealing with the community we dare not ignore any of the four aspects of its nature. We must treat it as a vital though changing whole, recognizing that changes in any single element will be reflected in all the others. Changes anywhere in the complex should lead us to anticipate changes elsewhere; modern social analysis can help us to predict what the changes will be and how they may be handled.

The delineation of the community area is a first concern of the pastor; he wants to know what space and population he is considering or should consider when he plans for his community. Indeed, unless he can come to some rather specific description of where his people live and what their characteristics are, he can scarcely hope to plan a local church program which will serve them, let alone help them in their community living. Information concerning certain conventionally or legally established areas is available to him on maps, though these may not reflect community boundaries at all. Such information includes the incorporated limits of the village if it is incorporated, the township in which the village lies, the school district, and the county. The school district and the county are more likely to be related to the community area than the former two, but community areas sometimes extend over more than one school district and across the boundaries of two or more counties. For further information, the pastor may write or visit the rural sociology department at the state university to see if it has made any recent social area studies which would involve his community.

Once the pastor has secured appropriate maps, he is in a position to determine boundaries on his own. With his maps, he can enlist the help of his laymen in business and the professions to determine how far their services extend into the countryside from the village center. If his church is located in the open country he will necessarily study the trading center toward which he finds himself and his people turning. Grocery trade will determine one area, hardware trade another, the bank will show a still larger area of influence as will the farm machinery dealer, the lumber yard operator, and the elevator manager. Little by little the maps will show a common area within which people are living together in the important details of their everyday lives. This common area of interrelationship is the community, operationally determined.

The question frequently troubles pastors as to whether or not the particular population center in which their church is located is a community center. Frank D. Alexander has worked with this problem as one of locality-group classification.[1] He suggests that each locality group be given a dual rating: first, a service rating "A" according to the following,

A_0 no services available,
A_1 1–4 services,
A_2 5–15 services,
A_3 16–49 services,
A_4 50–99 services,
A_5 100 or more services;

second, a group-identification rating "B",

B_0 No group identification,
B_1 Low group identification,
B_2 Medium group identification,
B_3 High group identification.

The "no group identification" category does not seem to make sense since, if persons do not identify with a

[1] "The Problem of Locality-Group Identification," *Rural Sociology*, September, 1952, pp. 236-44.

locality, there is no group. Alexander includes it, however, for theoretical completeness in dealing with a particularly impersonal service center.

A careful analytic description of the actual locality group in these terms helps us to see what measure of self-sufficiency it possesses. On that basis we can decide whether our living area tends to be a community or is rather a neighborhood within a larger community area. Obviously a locality group with a rating of A_2 or lower and a B_3 rating is at the neighborhood end of the continuum while B_1 or B_2 ratings with A_3 or above are well along the continuum toward community.

Karl A. Fox has turned to a more theoretical approach. He suggests that the community of tomorrow will involve an interrelationship between central cities and a much extended rural hinterland. He posits a grid pattern of roads and willingness on the part of farm families to travel an hour each way to do their trading. On this basis he divides the state of Iowa up into squares around central cities, which include all areas from which farmers can arrive in the central city with only an hour of driving at fifty miles an hour. He sees this unit, to which he gives the title "functional economic area," as the basic organizational and service unit for rural America tomorrow.

His discussion in Gore and Hodapp[2] makes room for smaller service centers nearer to the people and leaves the decision ultimately to technicians as to which level of service should be the organizing unit

[2] William J. Gore and Leroy C. Hodapp, *Change in the Small Community* (New York: Friendship Press, 1967), chapter 3, pp. 62-104.

for any particular activity. Whether churches can be organized effectively over such a large functional area involves a series of questions. What is important for the pastor to know is that such a suggestion has been seriously raised. Responsible leadership entails our giving serious consideration to this wider possibility. If we define the community in functional economic area terms, this suggests that we have given up the idea of personal psychological identification as a significant element in making a community.

Of what relevance is the community to the church, its work, and its pastor? First of all, the local community is the world which the church faces, with which it is hopefully engaged in a redemptive work. The world is more—much more—than the local community, but it is in the local community that contact with the world begins. Unless we are making a real and significant contact with men and women—all kinds of men and women—in the local community, we shall have precious little chance of making an impact of any kind upon the larger world of which our community is a part.

This local community is a microcosm of our total society. If the church is to witness to the world on the pressing social issues of our time, it must begin that witness in its own community area. It is easy to wax prophetically eloquent about the urban ghettos while we conveniently ignore the rural ghettos, the migrants' shacks, or the decaying homesteads of marginal farmers on poor land. Christians who become aware of their failures in their own local society and seek to make amends there will be open to prophetic preaching about

our total society. But the awareness of the need for
social witness on the part of churchmen must begin at
home—in the local community.

If the church is to be related to the world, it is
also to be related to other churches—to the fellowships
with which it so often has been in competition, if not
in conflict. And the community again becomes the most
appropriate and first level of ecumenical engagement.
In the local community the ecumenical task is most
difficult, since here theological and liturgical rationalizations can give respectability and support to
church groups which represent really social rather
than religious differences. Yet all talk about religious
oneness that cannot succeed in and among local persons where they live is talk and nothing more. It is
indeed true that national and international discussions
and agreements among the churches can clear away
outside interferences and rationalizations of local
church conflict, but the working together as Christians
regardless of confession or denominational fealty must
occur in the local living space of ordinary people—in
their own communities.

A third service which the community area provides
for the church is administrative. How shall we provide
ministerial leadership for town and country churches?
So far the local church has been the unit of our thinking. But many rural churches are small—so small indeed that they cannot provide a full-time position for
a trained pastor. Even when the financial resources
are available to support him, there is not enough work
to keep him busy. Many young ministers leave the
ministry because they are bored, because they do not

have enough to do to work with zest. A first rule should be that all work of any single denomination within a town and country community area, no matter how many local churches are involved, should be under the direction of a single pastor. Where more than one pastor is necessary, second and third pastors should be brought in not as pastors of individual churches but as members of a staff serving a parish which may be composed of a number of churches.

And this opens the door to the possibility of interdenominational cooperation in pastoral appointments. An ecumenical staff is a current possibility in many communities. Pastors from the constituent denominations might well become members of a joint staff serving all the churches without regard to denominational affiliation. Here as yet we have no sure guidelines except the guidelines of possibility. Local imagination can have free scope here and various degrees of shared authority and responsibility can become the basis of creative experimentation.[3]

It follows that the community can serve as the basis for church programming; it provides numbers of persons and resources of talent and wealth to mount programs which individual churches cannot manage. Specialized work with youth may well be carried out on a community rather than a single church basis. Study programs for women are often jointly planned with common literature on a national basis; why not carry them out in community terms locally? Imagination sets the only limits to cooperative programming in the daily

[3] Marvin Judy, *The Cooperative Parish in Nonmetropolitan Areas* (Nashville: Abingdon Press, 1967).

life of the churches. The community gives us a common base from which to work and a common audience to which we may address our message.

Finally, pastors who are always looking for an objective basis for evaluating the outreach of their churches find such a base in the community. Does the church membership come from and represent all areas of our community, all age-groups within the population of the community, all status groups therein? What of church participation? Is the representativeness we see on the books of the church belied in its pews on Sunday morning? Does the leadership of the church reflect all the segments of community life or do business men and wealthy farmers carry responsibilities which should with fairness be more widely shared? Does the giving of church people represent an adequate stewardship of their resources? All these questions come to us in a form which is answerable when we take the community area as a basis for judging the work of the church.

There is danger in giving as much attention as we have to the structure of the community. When the pastor finally draws a boundary line on the map, he is tempted to think that his work of community determination is completed. But communities are subject to all the forces of change which affect our common life in modern America. The lines which were boundaries last year may be overstepped this year so that the only safe perspective for the pastor is one of constant observation and continual survey and re-survey. The community area once established gives us a benchmark from which we can judge change and development, but it does not give us a fixed and final limit.

Rural sociologists in the study to which we have previously referred were asked to recommend books which, in their opinion, a rural pastor ought to read. More than any other volume they gave their votes to a community study of a central New York state town written by Arthur J. Vidich and Joseph Bensman and entitled *Small Town in Mass Society*.[4] Since this particular volume is so generally recommended, we may well consider its perspective in concluding our exploration of the term "community."

The thesis of the authors is succinctly phrased in the title: small towns preserve only an appearance of freedom and autonomy. They are really the subservient creatures of the larger society, and much of their public life constitutes an appearance of autonomy, which clothes their dependence and makes it acceptable to the citizenry. Politically, on the local and even on the county level, local people really have little power; the decisions are made in Albany or Washington and passed down. Economically the real power rests, not with the local independent businessman, but with the large manufacturer, the great banks, and such financial institutions as the insurance companies. Educationally the pattern is set by the demands of an alien larger society to which the majority of youth being educated in the local schools will eventually turn for a livelihood.

What of the churches? They indeed are local institutions run by local people—though by a very small number of them, it is true. They function not to give the

4 (Princeton: Princeton University Press, 1958).

local people any power but to provide support for the community self-image of independence and freedom. They function to make local dependence a little less evident, and therefore the plight of local people a little more tolerable. Whenever their ministers seek to speak objectively, they become *persona non grata;* congregations do not want their pastors to alert them to the real world, they want pastors who will make them comfortable in the real world by ignoring it as much as possible.

Sensitive pastors will recognize the accuracy of the Vidich-Bensman analysis. The situation as described is the way it is more often than we like to imagine. But need it be this way? Need the church provide a facade of acceptability and respectability for the slavery to mass society into which so many are falling? Or, if ministers are trained to pierce behind the facade and understand the real forces at work, can they help their people to see also, and to rediscover their own potential for freedom? Sociology gives us no answer to this question but it does make the question a reasonable one by helping us to see what is going on and instructing us in making reality clear to our people. The conviction that given the knowledge we can do something about the situation is our own adventure of faith.

6

The Power Structure

The power by which men survive is social power; there are animal species in which individuals exist for long periods of time in isolation and without reference to their kind, but man is not this kind of animal. His characteristic setting and resource, from the primitive hunting band of pre-historic peoples to the urban agglomerations of contemporary America, is the company of his fellows. His ability to persist in a hostile climate and environment is due not to his possession of unusual resistance to cold or heat or great strength; actually here his individual capacities are quite unimpressive. His survival hinges, rather, upon his capacity for teamwork, a capacity so subtle that it permits fellowship with our dead forbears whose counsel comes to us in that complex of skills and meanings which we denote as "culture."

An individual's birth is the culmination of one social relationship and thrusts him immediately into another social relationship, that of the family. His survival depends on someone's being willing to care for him, for as an infant he is completely unable to care for himself. His powerlessness means that from his birth others are exerting control over him; they assess his needs and provide the sustenance and shelter which they estimate he requires, so that his survival hinges upon the accuracy of their estimation of those requirements, the degree of their ability to provide for them, and their diligence in maintaining that provision on a dependable basis. If we survive infancy, it is because of the successful operation of a social group, actually, of a whole series of social groups.

All this suggests that human life begins with a built-in dependency in which survival is predicated upon the subordination of the newborn child to other more mature members of his species. And social life generally is built upon this pattern: all of us are, in essential details of our lives, dependent upon other persons, specialists who can do for us what we cannot do for ourselves. We think, of course, of such specialists as the doctor who provides understanding, diagnosis, and therapy when we are ill, or the lawyer who guides us through the legal labyrinth surrounding such necessary behaviors as buying a house or making a will. But we might equally think of such specialists as the trash collector or the filling station attendant whose constant ministries to us are essential prerequisites of civilized life in a technological society like ours.

Each of these specialists—indeed, each of us whenever we serve a specialized function in the division of labor—has some special measure of social power. The doctor isolates us from the members of our family in a hospital ward and permits no one to see us while proscribing our freedom of movement and behavior in a radical way. We accord him this power because of our faith that following his counsel will recover our health. We exchange our freedom and the companionship of family and friends for his knowledge and skill in healing us. The lawyer may order us not to speak or to refuse to answer questions which we would like to deal with in defense of our self-esteem, yet we remain silent because by so doing we can secure the benefits of his special skill and knowledge. It may appear that the trash collector has no special power, and this properly reflects the rural experience from which so many of us have come in which the disposition of life's refuse is a simple matter. But New Yorkers faced with a strike of trash collectors soon found how completely in the power of such men they are.

Each of us when he acts as a specialist is accorded a measure of social recognition. Many studies have been made of the relative prestige accorded the several occupational categories in our society. In a 1925 study in which 45 occupations were ranked by panels of experts, physicians ranked third and lawyers fifth, while street cleaners, the closest category to trash collector in that list, ranked forty-fourth with only ditch digger in a lower position. A 1963 National Opinion

Research Center study rated ninety occupations on the basis of a nation-wide sample of Americans. Physicians ranked second in the ratings, exceeded only by U.S. Supreme Court justices; lawyers ranked eleventh while garbage collectors ranked 88th, superior only to street sweepers and shoe shiners.[1]

Associated with prestige is privilege; generally men and women whose positions carry high prestige are also accorded many privileges, among them relatively higher incomes than the average, special emancipations from the duties weighing upon other citizens, special consideration in regard to particular legal regulations and requirements. The physician, for example, receives a higher income than most of us, is not required to serve on juries unless he wishes, and will not be prosecuted for driving faster than the speed limit or parking in an interdicted spot if in pursuit of his profession. However, in exchange for these privileges he is expected to carry out duties beyond the level of most of us: he is not limited to an eight-hour day or a forty-hour week, in emergency he must serve us regardless of our ability to pay or even our general worthiness, and he must expose himself to the risk of disease and infection in carrying out his work. The trash collector might be regarded as entirely unprivileged until we remember that his work hours and work week are strictly limited, so that his leisure time is in fact his own, while his job security is guaranteed by his civil service status.

[1] See discussion in Lee Taylor, *Occupational Sociology* (New York: Oxford University Press, 1968), p. 169-77.

Thus far, our illustrations have been taken from the world of work, an indication of how significant employment is for the social structure of our society. However, we need to stress the fact that the distribution of power, prestige and privilege is related to other factors than occupation: income, family background in a stable community, community participation, including participation in the church, and education are all significant differentiators of social power, prestige, and privilege. And we must also note that there is no absolute correlation between the categories of power and prestige and privilege. A policeman has great power, but in our culture certainly little prestige and almost no privileges, while a movie star may have great prestige and obtain many privileges but have little, if any, power.

Power in community is always relational and specific: it is the ability of one person or group to secure behavior in another person or group according to the purpose of the first party; and it is ability to do this in particular and specific situations. But a community, if it exists, is to some extent a unity, and therefore we should expect to find a pattern of generalized power within particular communities. Studies of social class or of stratification reveal that such structures or systems of power do in fact exist and can be charted. In general we may say that the top places in the pyramid of power will be occupied by persons of wealth, of education, and of long residence in the community. But this general pattern is considerably affected by the peculiar norms of the local community. In the American middle west in a county seat town the old family doctor who also serves on the board of directors of the local bank may be accorded almost dictatorial power where matters of health are concerned—in a flood with subsequent threat of epidemic, for example. On the other hand, in a mountain community in Appalachia the authority in such a case may devolve upon the preacher of the local sect, and townspeople may actively resist the efforts of state health officials to immunize the community on the insistence of their pastor that disease is a judgment of God, to seek to control disease is to defy God! In each community the set of prevailing norms determines the power figure and the action of the community.

Presently American sociologists are divided as to the method of determining community power structure and, consequently, present differing views as to what that structure is. On the one hand there is the reputational method of determining power figures and on the other the behavioral. Generally, practitioners of the first method arrive at the conclusion that the real power holders in the community are shadowy figures who operate behind the scenes and through puppets who dominate the life of the community in the interest of the retiring, and almost hidden, dominant figures. The picture tends to become a conspirational one with a few men or families of wealth and property prostituting the legitimate economic and political powers of the community to get their own way. Those who insist on surveying the actual operation of decisions in a community conclude that power operations tend to have a wider base and personnel, that men who are effective determinants of community action at one point are quite powerless at another.

It is clearly true that in a technologically sophisticated modern community the economically powerful are affected at every point by political and educational considerations which lead them to take an interest in and to try to influence political and educational decisions and political and educational leaders. On the other hand, it is equally apparent that this very need of support on the part of economically powerful persons gives to political and educational leaders in community affairs power that they did not previously possess. If someone needs me I at once possess a certain bargaining power with him: this insight has led many sociologists currently to develop an exchange theory of community power which catches up the truth in the apparently conflicting points of view previously maintained.

On occasion, pastors have canvassed their church memberships asking for detailed nominations of persons whom the members would like to see occupying the positions of leadership in the church. Whenever this is done, it is a surprising result that many more people are acceptable to their fellow members in leadership positions than we think. If a few persons continue to occupy the key positions, it is not because others are not available in the membership to do the jobs successfully; nor is it necessarily because officeholders wish to hang on to their jobs. It is often because the lethargy of habit and custom keeps us from exploring alternate patterns of leadership. The power system of the church is more susceptible to alteration than we think. It is a fact that in all too many churches and communities key positions are held by a few power figures. But that this is a necessary situation or one not subject to adjustment is simply not proved. Where an entrenched officeholder seeks to maintain this regime because of his own inner needs for recognition and authority, studies show that the church or other group moves forward to a new level of efficiency and subjective satisfaction when the dictator is displaced and a widely based leadership is established. People do not like to be dominated; they enjoy directing their own lives.

If we wish to define the community power-structure in a particular local community, we have an objective basis for doing so. First, we need to get something of a cross section of the community personnel. For this, a list of the voters is probably the best source, though by no means an infallible or complete one. From the list we can select every tenth name or every twentieth, so that we will get a sample of approximately fifty names. Type each name on a separate three-by-five-inch card, thus developing a representative list of community citizens to be evaluated by their fellows.

The second step is to choose and enlist the service of a panel of community informants, people who represent various age and economic segments of the community and who have lived therein long enough to be somewhat familiar with the community's patterns of power. A typical panel might include a high school youth, a housewife, a farmer, a business or professional man, a laborer and a retired person. The panel members are interviewed separately and in a private situation where each will feel free to talk, uninhibited by the presence of anyone but the interviewer. Each person is presented with the file of fifty cards containing the names and asked to sort through the pack in order to arrange together those persons who belong together in the community. People who belong together are placed in piles together and thus the informant produces a series of piles of cards, each pile containing names of people who are essentially similar. Meanwhile the interviewer notes any stated basis for discrimination and any observations the informant may make in the sorting process. At the conclusion of the work he asks what relationship the separated piles have to one another and arranges them in order of the informant's preferences. Thus there emerges a division of the sample into superior and inferior categories which can be numbered with "one" as the highest and thence downward in sequence to the most inferior category.

A master chart or table with the names of the sample of citizens listed in the left margin and the initials of the informants listed across the top is used to enter the judgment of each panel member. If the member makes four groupings, a rating of one to four is entered after each name in the sample. If the citizen is unknown to the informant, then an "X" is entered. When the judgments of all the informants are entered, the ratings may be added across for each person in the sample and divided by the number of informants rating that person to get his average score. The fact that one informant develops only three categories while another develops five need not interfere with the averaging, since what we are after anyway is the general weighting of persons in the community and not any arbitrary score. If certain individuals are consistently given a higher rating by the informants, we will have identified persons high in the structure of power. Failure among the informants to agree may mean that we have no community. A sharp cleavage of opinion indicates a divided or polarized community.

A second method of determining community power structure involves the use of the "Index of Status Characteristics" developed by Lloyd Warner and his associates and described in Warner, Meeker and Eels' *Social Class in America*.[2] This method rates the same fifty persons on four objective determiners of position: occupation, source of wealth, house type, and neighborhood. On each of these determiners a rating of from one to seven is given corresponding to the best in any category down to the worst. A complicated weighting system is then applied to the assembled data to give to each person an Index of Status Characteristics. This index provides a picture of the particular community in comparison with other American communities, as well as an assessment of each citizen's position with which we can compare our previous ratings derived from our panel of informants. Discrepancies will appear between the ratings of persons arrived at by the two systems, and these discrepancies will, of course, require further study and interpretation. The pastor who wishes to make use of this second method will find, in the textbook referred to above, tables and charts on which to base his analysis.[3]

[2] *Ibid.*
[3] *Ibid.*, pp. 122-29, 185.

When the data is in and analyzed, the pastor will wish to see whether in the church membership and in his ministry all the segments of this pyramid of power are represented. Do the same persons dominate the church who dominate the community? Is the correlation with wealth positive or are there other discriminating factors which local people take into account? Such a study will alert the pastor to realities in his church situation which he may otherwise miss altogether.

The sensitive pastor is bound to face the question we raised earlier in reference to Vidich and Bensman's study, *Small Town in Mass Society*. Does the local community structure of power have any autonomy to regulate and direct the community's life and development, or are local community power figures simply front men for the domination of local people by the military-industrial complex or whatever "establishment" is currently identified as ruling? The question stated as such is badly put, for it is obvious that technology has made us one society and one world. A better way of stating the problem is to ask what the alternatives are among which local people may choose. In an area of declining population, the churches obviously have a limited number of options, but it is important that those options be clearly stated. Churches can continue to maintain their autonomy as personnel and wealth diminish, spending more and more on the maintenance of the institution and less and less on outreach and service. They can demand more and more by way of gifts and service from the fewer and fewer that remain, with less and less to show from this heroic sharing of diminished resources. Or they can discover ways of combining resources and maintaining services without focus on the maintenance of the usual congregational arrangements. Freedom and autonomy exist, not in the possibility of unlimited choices but rather, in a sensing of what the viable choices are and a creative and imaginative selecting among them.

7

Community Decision-making

Pastors, along with other professionals in town and country communities, are concerned to discover how individuals come to accept new ways of doing things, as well as how groups and communities themselves change their ways. Much of a pastor's time is spent in helping men and women make those changes in their lives which are demanded by new situations or altered circumstances. He is required as well to help church groups, churches themselves, and even communities develop programs adjusted to the demands our changing times place upon them. Often we talk about conversion as if a change is easily and readily made once its value is impressed upon a person. Or we act as if to present a new and reasonable plan to the church board is sufficient ground for getting it accepted. To adopt this attitude is to ignore the nature of the human material with which we work. It is as important to understand the tensions and strains that affect men and women in building a new sanctuary as it is for the architect to know the strains and stresses to be put upon his building materials by wind, weather, and use.

For some thirty years now, rural sociologists have been studying the decision-making process, sometimes speaking of diffusion, on other occasions using the phrase "practice-adoption." They have charted, for example, the sequence of knowledge and attitude by which a person moves from his first acquaintance with a new farm practice to his eventual adoption of it. Research of this type has produced a body of generalized knowledge which can be applied to all sorts of decision-making. In addition to the work done in the field of adoption of new farm practices, studies have been made, to a lesser degree, in the field of health practices, the use of new drugs in health care, and the acceptance of new religious practices.

When a new farm practice—the use of a particular new weed killer, for example—becomes available to working farmers, a particular farmer will pass through five definable stages from knowledge to adoption. The first stage is commonly referred to as "awareness"; he discovers that a new method of dealing with his weed problem exists. He may read about it in his farm paper, hear it over the radio or television, learn about it in a discussion with the farm adviser or the salesman for the chemical company, or listen in on talk about it as he gossips with his neighbors in the coffee shop uptown. Certainly in one or another or perhaps all of these ways it comes to his attention that he can deal with weeds in a fashion different than the one he now uses.

If weeds constitute a pressing problem to him, he moves to the second stage: "interest." Now he is not a passive listener, but is actively seeking information on this new practice. His procedure at the interest stage will be governed a great deal by his general patterns of perception. He may only talk to his neighbors and friends, or he may write to the state university extension service for information or consult in detail with the technicians of the chemical company. In characteristic ways he tries to discover all he can about the nature of the new weed control practice. He is out to inform himself.

The third stage, called "evaluation," is the period in which the farmer asks himself: "What will using this practice mean to me?" Involved is an assessment of costs and returns: Is the new weed killer more expensive than the old? Is an adaptation of present machinery possible or is an investment in new machinery required for its use? Does its use carry with it long-term effects which might limit the flexibility of my farm operation? Does its use hinge on favorable weather so that heavy wet weather or a prolonged dry spell limits its effectiveness? What effect does this chemical have on wild life? And these are only a beginning of the many significant questions which the working farmer will ask as he evaluates the new procedure in relationship to his particular farm operation.

If the evaluation proves positive, the farmer moves

on to a fourth stage: "trial." At this point in the adoption process, he actually makes a preliminary and tentative use of the new weed killer on his own farm. He very probably selects one field, perhaps a field plagued with problem weeds, arguing, "If it will do any good here, its worth using." He has not yet committed himself to the new process and product, but he is giving it a chance to demonstrate its superiority to his current practice. If it does demonstrate clear and distinct superiority, he moves to the final stage: "adoption." When he adopts the new practice, the farmer dispenses with his former procedures and makes the new process his standard practice.

Not all persons adopt a new practice with the same speed; students have described typical categories of persons in relationship to the pace of adoption: innovator, early adopter, early majority, late majority, and laggard. As we move from innovator to laggard we move from the young, well-educated, wealthy farmer with a large acreage and cosmopolitan interests to the older, less educated, poor farmer on a small farm with only local contacts and references. At the extreme the innovator seems to welcome novelty for its own sake while the laggard seems to treasure the old and familiar for its own sake. Both, however, and this is particularly important for pastors to understand, require time in the adoption process. Even innovators adopt through stages and over time; they differ from the laggard significantly only in their much earlier and more rapid adoption movement.

Different categories of adopters use different sources of information, and all categories use different sources of information at the different stages in the adoption process. The mass media are important at the awareness stage, but their impact becomes less the closer a person moves to adoption. Technical information from the extension service and the sales personnel are more widely used by innovators and early adopters than by the other categories. Neighbors, relatives, and friends are more important in the adoption process for all but innovators and early adopters. From these facts it is obvious that resources and influences which get a new process or program accepted by one category of persons will need to be altered or adjusted when we are dealing with another category. The pastor who wishes his members to adopt a new religious practice or program must determine into what categories his members fall before he can select the informational media and the leadership patterns that will reach and move them.

There is evidence that the general atmosphere of a neighborhood or community will affect the openness of its members to new ideas and practices. If the general mood of a neighborhood is one of satisfaction with things as they are, or resignation in bad situations from which there seems to be no escape, a pastor should expect to find similar attitudes governing the reactions of his lay leaders to new program suggestions or adjustments within the church. Laymen do not leave their basic mind-sets outside the church when they come to a board meeting on religious matters. We must sense and understand the community's basic attitude in order to work fruitfully within the Christian fellowship.

So far we have been discussing the ways in which individual persons decide to adopt a new practice, though the heading of the chapter is "Community Decision-making." A pastor will remember that in discussing the community we pointed out that a community, whatever else it may involve, is, first of all, persons. It follows then that we shall not be in a position to understand how a community acts until we know something about how persons act when faced with the challenge of novelty and change. I do not mean that community change is individual change writ large; that emphatically is not the case, But I do mean that processes which we understand from our analysis of the individual's decision-making have a part in the development of decisions on a group level.

Let us take an actual case. A young pastor moved to an old and strong parish in Iowa as his first full-time assignment. He found a substantial church property well cared for but lacking in space and equipment appropriate to the educational work of the church. At the same time he found such numbers of children and youth involved in the church school program that it was almost physically impossible to accommodate them, let alone provide an environment in which teachers could do anything but shout to make themselves heard. He carefully tabulated numbers of children and youth by age, indicated that an increase in the number of younger families promised to make the supply of children not less but greater, developed a statement of the standards for housing classes in terms of square feet of floor space per pupil, outlined the necessary amenities related to teaching, and confidently presented his report to the church governing board. The members heard him out with real interest and appreciation, received his report with thanks, and passed on to other business. It was quite clear that they intended to do nothing whatever about it.

Where had he failed? This was the question that haunted the young pastor. He went over his tables and charts and found them clear and attractive, yet obviously their meaning to his church board was quite different from their meaning to him. He felt certain that his presentation had offended none of them, that no one felt that his prerogatives had been usurped or his authority challenged; indeed, he felt certain that there was no opposition to his perspective and suggestions at all. Rather, there was no concrete and immediate disposition to act. This lack of motive he simply could not understand.

As a faithful pastor he maintained the denominational tradition of regular calling on the shut-ins of the parish. Among those to whom he so ministered was an aged couple still living in their farm home, though they left the farm operation itself to a neighboring son-in-law. As the pastor made his regular monthly call on this husband and wife he found himself talking with them on the materials he had presented to the church board. He spoke of the confusion of tongues in church school due to the utterly inadequate physical plant available, of the increasing burden of enrollment because of the burgeoning youth in young families (with which they were familiar through their own grandchildren), of what the church might and should provide by way of room and equipment in order to share with these youngsters the good news of Christ. The old people were a most emotionally satisfying audience reciprocating his information with questions, objections, alternatives, problems. The pastor found himself stopping by whenever he was in their vicinity to chat about his concerns for the church as much to relieve his own pent-up discouragement as to minister to the aged couple. It was fun to talk with them; they found it fun, too, for it made them a part of the on-going church again.

Some six months later at a regular board meeting a middle-aged layman asked the privilege of making a presentation. It seemed that he had become concerned about the lack of appropriate facilities for the church school; he discussed the problem with rough but real insight based on information; he ended by moving that the board establish a building committee to plan for new facilities for Christian education. The pastor sat by dumbfounded while a second layman seconded the motion, and the board, after interested discussion, voted unanimously to move ahead. What he had suggested six months earlier without any apparent impact was now in process of being achieved without any intervention on his part at all! Furthermore, this was no mere flash-in-the-pan, for a most suitable structure was in fact built with commendable speed.

In assaying the reasons behind this happy outcome, the pastor noted an important one immediately, the factor of time. We have seen that the adoption of a new practice by a farmer or a family involves consideration over time. To have expected his board to have acted immediately on his presentation would have been unrealistic; the members needed time to sort out their impressions, to answer their own doubts and questions, to consider resources and plans. And time is a factor in community decision-making. No group is ready to reach an important decision the first time the issue is presented. To force an early decision is to guarantee either the rejection of the proposition or, if the pastor uses sufficient pressure from his office and status, a hesitant acceptance which will not involve the sort of active and financial support that a project eventually must achieve.

What the young pastor did not so clearly see at first was the role of the aged couple and his interviews with them in the decision-making process. Though these old people could never attend church, their children were active in all its aspects. Sunday noon all the children and grandchildren regularly repaired to the ancestral home for Sunday dinner. Around the dinner table the old parents presented, and the whole family discussed, what the pastor had previously said in his call. And from this web of interaction discussion spread out through children and grandchildren to the entire parish. The man who made the motion in the board was a son-in-law and the seconder was a nephew. What had previously been a clever idea of the pastor's —and isn't every pastor expected to have clever but impractical ideas?—had become, in this process of family and neighborhood interaction, a parish project. It no longer belonged to the preacher, it belonged to the church.

This illustration introduces us to types of persons who play their part in any decision reached by the group. The pastor served as an "innovator"; an innovator is frequently an outsider, as most pastors are, at least early in their ministries; he sees problems in situations local people accept because things have always been that way; he brings a wider horizon of expectation and possibility to bear upon those problems. Often he is the first to recognize a problem in the local parish and to suggest needs and remedies to the congregation. But the pastor-innovator alone is helpless to develop a parish or community decision for change; helpless, that is, unless he knows how to ally other leaders with himself in developing change.

The aged parents were "key-communicators," [1] or "legitimizers." [2] They were a focal point in any serious attempt to distribute information and their interest in the matter carried a sort of local *imprimatur;* among church people their concern meant that this was something to be thought about. Other family members were "diffusers," they carried the discussion wherever they went and with whomever they came in contact; they sensed the reactions of others, met their objections, heard and responded to incipient opposition until, when it was time to make a motion, the disposition of the parish was clear and the support for the building program guaranteed. The pastor's calls on his aged parishioners had started a process of decision-making which issued in the formal vote of the board

[1] Herbert F. Lionberger, *Adoption of New Ideas and Practices* (Ames: Iowa State University Press, 1960), p. 55.

[2] George M. Beal et al., *Social Action and Interaction in Program Planning* (Ames: Iowa State University Press, 1966), p. 81, 82.

and its implementation through committees, architectural explorations, financial campaign, and the actual construction itself.

Rate of change varies from community to community and from issue to issue. Changes that are not costly economically or in terms of local group arrangements are more apt to be accepted quickly than their more expensive counterparts. In some communities, as we have earlier pointed out, an atmosphere hospitable to change and newness exists, and in such communities new programs get an early hearing. In others a satisfaction with things as they are may make any change suspect. The value system of a group determines the relative acceptability of new ways: if people generally regard sickness as a divine punishment, they will not readily accept the Salk vaccine in the prevention of infantile paralysis; indeed, to seek to escape polio will be interpreted by persons holding such a theology as tempting God.

Again it is perfectly possible for a group to accept a change, at least so far as its externals are concerned without accepting it rationally. A specialist in an underdeveloped country succeeded in persuading villagers to dig more than one hundred irrigation wells before he realized that they were not using the water for the irrigation of their crops. When he sought to understand why they did not use it, he learned that they felt there was something unnatural about such underground water, that it was not appropriate to the growth of plants, that it might even poison the plants if it were applied. Indeed this expert succeeded in getting his program carried out, but he did not succeed in improving the village agricultural development.

We may summarize the process of community decision-making thus:

1. Effective decisions for change in any group involve a period of time;
2. Members of a group serve different functions in the decision process;
3. The processes thus differentially served are:
   a. Innovation,
   b. Legitimation,
   c. Diffusion,
   d. Evaluation,
   e. Decision,
   f. Implementation;
4. Failure to deal with any part of the process threatens the entire development; and
5. All elements of the process may move through formal channels, but frequently important aspects may and do occur informally.

Change within a community moves according to a pattern; the same pattern governs change in a group within a community such as a church or an American Legion local. If the pastor has some understanding of this pattern, he will have more perception of what is occurring within the community and be better able to assist the forces of change and growth.

8

Communication

Communication is a basic and constant element in human relationships; almost any act invites, objects to, or questions the act or anticipated act of another person. Our communication may be intentional, as when we beckon to another person as an invitation to join us. Often, however, a given meaning is unintended but inferred by others, as when a certain stiffness in manner warns another off: that the stiffness is a posture of weariness and not of intention does not prevent it from creating an impression of aloofness. Such ambiguity is a constant of all attempts at communication: to make what we intend and what we convey as nearly one as possible is both the aim and the art of communication.

While communicative behavior is not limited to man

but is widely shared by other species, man is the communicator *par excellence*. He alone has elaborated primitive gesture, sign, and signal into the complicated vocabularies of formal language. With man alone do words become significant referents to, and finally substitutes for, objects and acts. When we give names to objects and to ways of behaving toward them, we develop a control over our environment such as no other species has achieved. Our cooperation with others of our kind is no longer limited to acts which we can describe in gestures, upon objects to which we can point. With words we can locate a tree at a road intersection a mile away and instruct a fellow human to look at it in admiration, to climb it for fun, or to cut it down for fuel.

Language obviously is a product of society, not only of the current society in which we learn it, but of that society's extension into the past. Language changes, develops, and grows, but it begins for any of us as an inheritance from past generations of men. And the learning of language is a social process: family members around him shape the child's primitive vocalizations into the family's pattern of pronunciation and meaning. English parents shape the child's verbalizations to an English accent and vocabulary, French parents develop the same basic organic equipments in their own characteristic and different manner. How basic these fundamental influences are is demonstrated by the difficulty Americans have in pronouncing the German "ch" or the equal difficulty experienced by Germans in managing the English "th." The basic functioning of the physiological organism has been so completely shaped in a particular way that its flexibility is substantially diminished.

To be useful as a means of communication, words must have precise meanings that are generally understood and accepted by the society in which the words are used. But modern communities sharing a common language include numerous societies: English is the language of Great Britain, Ghana, India, and the United States, to name only a few of the countries which carry on their conversation officially in English. But the meaning of English words may be quite different in these several English-speaking societies. And within each of them are a number of subsocieties with peculiar and specialized vocabularies: thus, in the United States we are aware of the specialized vocabulary of the homosexual world, the argot of the street gang, the highly stylized speech of the "beat" and "hippie" communities and, to note a quite different kind of specialization, the language of the clinic and the hospital. Our success as communicators hinges in large measure on our capacity to have some understanding of these specialized vocabularies.

Ordinarily we distinguish two meanings for any given word: denotative and connotative. The object or process to which a particular word specifically refers is its "denotation." The atmosphere, the impression, the emotional evaluation which the word produces is its "connotation." Frequently, failure to differentiate between denotative and connotative meanings of words involves us in confusion and futile argument.

Many discussions of the rural church and rural life illustrate the confusion which results when we do not carefully distinguish between denotation and connotation. "Rural" has a very specific meaning in terms of the United States Census. It refers to persons living in population divisions of less than 2,500 persons which are not adjacent to or in contiguous development with a city of 50,000 or more. In 1970 the number of our citizens that belonged in this category was 26.5 percent. But the connotation of rural for many is backward, living in primitive housing without electricity or sanitary conveniences, largely engaged in agriculture, relatively uneducated, and little interested in the amenities of civilized life. Accordingly, students who are impressed with the cultural advantages now available to all Americans through new means of transportation and communication often make the statement: "There are no rural people in the U.S.A. anymore." Using a conventional connotation of "rural," they make a judgment which is quite inaccurate if we use the term "rural" in its denotative sense. Such discussion scarcely informs or enlightens.

It is quite as possible to attach a positive meaning to the word "rural." Protagonists of rural church and community interests often identify "rural" with honest, straightforward, hard-working, friendly, eager to help those in distress, loyal to friends, courageous, outspoken, independent, and freedom-loving. These are their connotations for the term. Urban, by way of contrast, tends to become associated with all the opposite qualities, and heaven is seen as a bright and shiny small town writ large. If our arguments start from this connotation rather than the specific denotation of less than 2,500 population, we shall be debating with much feeling but no sense. "Rural" as "urban" is neither all good nor all bad, as any pastor knows who has taken seriously the doctrine of original sin. "Rural" as a denotative term we can use with profit; "rural" as a normative judgment only confuses our conversations.

We have, then, three obvious sources of confusion in communication growing out of the nature of words themselves. (1) Two persons may fail to make sense to one another because their denotative definition of particular words is different. Or (2) they may fail to understand one another because the connotation specific words have for them is not the same. (3) They also may fail to understand the message each has for the other because one is using the word in its denotative sense and the other in its connotative. Many differences may be clarified by determining that we share common definitions of terms and are using the terms as defined and not with connotative overtones. Precise and commonly accepted and understood definitions of the terms of discussion are the essential prelude to significant communication.

A first step each pastor should take in his community if he is concerned both to communicate meaningfully with his people and to help them communicate with one another is to understand his own reference group in terms of vocabulary. We must become self-conscious at the point of whose definitions are normative for us. Since pastors are mobile persons coming into the local community from outside, they have acquired their word usage from other than the local groups they serve. The earliest and most fundamental source of our definitions and particularly of the connotations of terms is our family of origin. Our parents and siblings have given us our most fundamental meanings: are these representative of the educational, economic, and social level of the persons we serve? Both university and seminary fellowships have left their marks upon our vocabulary, influences that only a few of our local church members share. The ecclesiastical fellowship of which we are members marks us, too; we reflect the thinking and concerns of our fellow pastors in the use of words. The whole involved language of theology has a special technical and academic meaning to us while it may possess an experiential meaning for local churchmen quite at variance with out understandings. We also need to consider the generation to which we belong; recent studies of pastoral attitudes and opinions indicate that age is the variable most significantly related to differences in basic orientation.[1]

In this connection we should note that the pastor's difficulty in entering his church and community as an outsider is becoming the problem of an ever-increasing number of Americans. We have always been a people on the move, as witness the westward expansion and then the city-ward movement of the nineteenth and early twentieth centuries. But now military adventure and the bureaucratic pattern of big business shifting its personnel around the country and world have made

[1] Murray H. Leiffer, *Changing Expectations and Ethics in the Professional Ministry* (Evanston: Bureau of Social and Religious Research, 1969).

S. Burkett Milner, "Lay and Clergy Expectations of the Ministry" (Unpublished Ph.D. Thesis, Northwestern University, 1970).

us a restless people. Many of our parishioners are trying to speak to their neighbors in a vocabulary which they learned in a quite different societal setting. A Methodist from rural Pennsylvania, newly settled in Southern California, will have to relearn his theological vocabulary if he is to survive as a Methodist. He may find it simpler to unite with a sectarian group in which his literalistic and legalistic theological vocabulary remains current rather than remain a Methodist. Confusion within church and community affairs is in part due to the fact of our constant mobility as Americans. It is therefore important for us to help our people discover something of the background of their particular use of language, at least to call their attention to the possibilities of misunderstanding implicit in differing backgrounds.

When the pastor has become self-conscious regarding his own word usage, he is in a position to take a second necessary step: to identify the subgroups with different vocabularies in the local community where he serves. Are there significant age-group differentiations? Do occupational groups have specialized vocabularies? Are there ethnically oriented groups with special ways of speaking? Social classes often, though not universally, develop characteristic vocabularies with connotational differences. An exploration of the significant local reference groups will put the pastor in a position at least to recognize, and partially to understand, difference in word meaning.

Groups whose members suffer from discrimination are apt to have a particularly difficult vocabulary from the point of view of the outsider. Persons discriminated against attach secretly shared connotations to words with apparently innocent and common meanings and apply these terms to those who discriminate against them. Thus the supposed inferior person is able to make uncomplimentary comments regarding members of the oppressing class in their presence to members of his own class. Through a specialized vocabulary he asserts his own dignity and independence at the expense of those who regard themselves as his betters and who have the power to punish him for open insolence. A pastor cannot expect early in his ministry in a community to master this special language but, if he is aware it exists, he can beware of thinking he knows what is being communicated in a conversation between members of the subordinate class.

After we have determined our own language bias and identified the several language subgroups in our community, we are in a position to help in communication between the several parties. We will be able to anticipate communication difficulties when members of alien subgroups attempt to speak to one another, and to interject in discussion a question regarding the meaning of a specific term to the parties who are using it. The very effort to explain meanings to others brings an atmosphere of sanity and reasonableness to what might otherwise be a shouting match, for to explain something to another requires that we think about it ourselves. And as pastors we must be ready to explain our own meanings, too, a difficult thing for a pastor to accept when the words under question are theological; for what is theological shorthand with us (an easy means of covering a lot of ground fast to arrive at the crux of an argument) may be and indeed is only confusing to the alert but unindoctrinated mind.

Thus far we have dealt with language as a means of communication and so it is, the single most effective means we have. But we would indeed fail in complete understanding if we neglected to take into account the noncommunicative functions of language. Many times what is said serves some other purpose than that of communication and to treat it literally would only lead to confusion.

For one thing, we use language for expressive purposes. "Amen" and "hallelujah" are words of joy and praise not meant to convey a message to others but to express emotional experience. Of course "amen" may in fact simply mean that the prayer is over or the benediction ended, and "hallelujah" may be merely rote response to a preacher's excess of oratory. So we conventionalize great ecstatic words. But the essential meaning of such words is the indication of an inner state, indeed, not so much its indication as its direct expression. Such words in their proper usage are not far from the glossolalia of the speaker in tongues.

Now many ordinary words are used in an expressive fashion. Minority representatives in our day, whether they be black or young or radical, make "demands." That word grates on the sensitivities of many of us who grew up in a more urbane generation. But the usage of the term is very largely expressive, an assertion of the essential adulthood and dignity of the ones who use it. Children, they say, ask or petition for favors but adults demand what they want. Another fashionable expressive word is "reparations"; to point out that the denotation of that work makes it inapplicable in the contemporary situation is a useless exercise in lexicography. "Reparations" is an expression of the deep sense of being wronged which those who use the term feel. It is expressive language.

Expressive language always calls for acceptance of its user by those to whom it is addressed. It does not call for argument. To accept "demands" with dignity and concern is to meet the man who makes them on his own field. To accept him does not necessarily mean to grant his demands specifically or in toto; but it does mean to take seriously his assertion of his own worth as a man. When and if he feels this acceptance, he will no longer need to use this particular brand of expressive language. But to take his language seriously is essential if we are to take him seriously. Expressive language does in fact communicate, but on a different level than rational discourse.

Language may also be used defensively, that is, not to communicate but to hide something. When we have something we wish to conceal we may talk a great deal. Our talk is a kind of smoke screen behind which we protect the revelation we fear may be disclosed. Rationalization is the process by which we assign respectable reasons to explain conduct which is basically motivated by considerations we do not want known. Here language becomes not a means of but a barrier to communication.

To identify and then to deal with the defensive use of language is a most difficult process. Such defensiveness cannot be successfully overcome in frontal encounter. If one of us feels he has to use words to defend himself, he is uncertain and afraid; hence, our first effort must be to move the conversation into an area in which he no longer feels threatened. In ensuing encounter he may develop enough confidence in others of us and then in himself to dispense with defenses and to use words genuinely. But he will not do so until he no longer feels threatened by an open communication of himself.

To this defensive use of language we churchmen have contributed. In stressing the importance of moral righteousness we have failed to take realistic account of our own perversity. We are none of us perfect beings, yet the insistence with which we, as pastors, emphasize the importance of goodness—seen as conventionally respectable behavior—has put many of us under pressure to appear to be what we are not. Now the church and its pastors ought not to encourage immoral conduct, of course; but we ought to be ready to recognize and admit that all of us alike are subject to pressures and temptations to evil. If we acknowledge our own temptations and failures, it becomes less necessary for any of us to make a defensive curtain of our language. And incidentally, when we frankly admit our temptations, we put ourselves in a position to deal with them openly and realistically. And others can then listen to and help us.

The preacher is preeminently a talker; words are his stock in trade. He owes it to himself and to his people to make an honest stewardship of the communication process. His awareness of the obstacles to communication and of the noncommunicative uses of language will help him in his own effort to "preach the Word" and in encouragement of others to speak honestly. Communication is socially framed, from our perception of what the other is presenting through our response to that perception in word or act. Throughout the process are possibilities for misunderstanding and irrelevant response. The pastor who makes himself a more accurate communicator and helps his people to say what they mean is a true "minister of the Word."

9

Role

In prior discussions, particularly those dealing with community, the power-structure, and decision-making, we have indicated that we all occupy positions in society which are, in fact, relationships with other persons and with the social whole. Each of us is involved in varied relationships to other persons or categories of persons: we are husbands in relation to our wives, fathers in relation to our children, neighbors in relation to the family next door, citizens vis-à-vis the state, pastors in the service of the church, and so the list might be indefinitely extended. In all of these positions or statuses (a term we shall analyze in detail in a later chapter) we play characteristic roles, that is, adopt socially defined patterns of behavior. Society has set certain expectations and developed specific norms in terms of which we are expected to behave in these particular relationships. A "role," then, is a pattern of normative conduct related to a particular social relationship.

Roles grow out of such differentiating characteristics as sex, age, kinship, and occupation. A role is a prescription for behavior, a standard of practice in a given relationship. It is never a private invention but always a social definition. As we shall note in the process of our discussion, however, persons play out their roles in elaborations which give scope to their personal and unique capacities as well as to the social norms. Whenever I make contact with a stranger or a strange group, my first effort is to identify him or it so as to determine my role, my responsibilities for behavior. At first my overtures or my responses to overtures are tentative and uncertain, but as I more clearly identify the stranger, my attitudes and conduct become more clear, specific, and confident. I learn what part I am to play, what my role is to be.

In a static or stable society, the several roles which a single person plays are coherent with one another and tend to bring an essential unity to his personal life. Being a man, a husband, a father, a hunter, and a priest all fit together; the norms and expectations governing each role tend to mesh with and give support to the norms and expectations governing other roles. The essential unity of the society provides an established unity for the person who is a member of it. Indeed, such a person is scarcely aware of moving from one role to another.

But in a dynamic society there is no such guarantee of unity between roles; indeed we can be sure that the several roles we are called on to play will have norms in conflict with one another. To take the familiar and apparently compatible roles of wife and mother in our society as an example, a woman may well find herself in serious personal conflict as she attempts to discharge the responsibilities of both roles as they are popularly defined in middle class America. As a wife she is required to play a companionate role with and to her husband; she is always to be personally well-groomed and attractive, ready to enter into his activities both business and recreational, at least potentially as free and mobile as he is so that she can come when he calls, and must be informed on a wide variety of public matters so that she can converse with him about his interests and, if need be, keep him up to date on such matters of knowledge as distinguish the cultured person. But as a mother she is the administrator of an intricate enterprise, housing, clothing, feeding, and nurturing her growing children. Familial life grinds to a halt if mother is not available with the family station wagon to chauffeur the children to their manifold engagements, to do the shopping on which the family nutrition depends, and to represent the family at parent-teacher meetings or in the scout organization. Obviously two such demanding roles do not fit together: a woman might well wreck her health, if not her sanity, by trying to be efficient in meeting the norms of both. Yet if she does not meet those conflicting norms to her own satisfaction she must regard herself as a failure, since she feels this is what her society expects of her. Whether others do in fact criticize her failures is beside the point; thinking they do, she condemns and rejects herself.

In the above illustration we have a case of role conflict, in which the tension is induced by extreme demands on the person's time and effort. There are other role conflicts in which differing roles demand contradictory ways of behaving, that is, are normatively in conflict. A case in point would be the conflict experienced by a teenage gang member. His family sets certain standards of behavior regarding the use of the family car, all having to do with the preservation of the car and of the young man. His fellows in the gang, however, view a car as an expendable item in the pursuit of adventure. To negotiate a tricky stretch of road with speed and flourish rather than with safety is their norm; and so the teenager is caught between two conflicting role expectations. He may try to fulfill both, keeping his fingers crossed in the hope that he can bring the family car home unscarred, and avoid any run-in with the traffic police. But this may seem too risky to him in the light of anticipated parental sanctions, in which case he may turn to stealing cars with which to perform adventurously, using the family car only for getting around town in sober fashion. What should be clear to us is that in such a conflict of roles there is no really satisfactory answer, for the same social forces that pressure the teenager to be a "good" boy at home pressure him to be a "bad" boy with the gang. In each case he is conforming to a specific group norm. And he may attempt to reconcile conflicting norms between home and gang by indulging in behavior which violates a third set of norms, those of the community.

Thus far we have dealt with interrole conflicts but our human situation is further compounded by the possibility of intra-role conflicts. We are all familiar with the fact that conflict between husband and wife leads to conflict within the personalities of their children. The children's behavior reflects the inconsistent expectations set by warring parents. Without a consistent role pattern of son or daughter, the child is constantly working against himself. Out of such intra-role conflict he may learn to deceive, to rebel, or to retreat. He will not learn, however, to play well the role of a son, a key role on which the competent performance of so many other roles depends.

Within the role the pastor plays in the community there may be real inconsistencies: can the minister successfully serve as the nurturing pastor to his people and also bring prophetic judgment to the sins of the church and community? Many of us have struggled with this dilemma and have found no easy resolution. The issue here is not one of moral or intellectual failure on the pastor's part; it is rather the complexity of our expectations of the pastoral office. We feel torn and divided, because the expectation to which we react is an intricate one: to be a good minister necessitates on occasion that we behave with apparent inconsistency, because we are responding to superficially divergent expectations.

A further complication occurs when the definition of the pastor's role varies between laymen and minister. And here the tensions are often compounded by the fact that laymen and minister belong to different age categories with differing needs coloring their interpretations of the pastor's role. For a young man, and many rural pastors are young men just beginning their ministries, the future development of the church and the community is of preeminent concern. But often the church governing board is composed of men and women in their sixties and older; their future concerns are conditioned by approaching death, a fact which they may not recognize but which governs their perception of the future none the less. For them the future is of another world so that they look to their pastor as a guide to that next world; whereas their pastor's future and hence his interests are very much in this world. Their sense of need and his perception of need are governed by different life settings; the generation gap—if and when there is a generation gap—is a difference in priorities growing out of a difference in definitions of the future. It is not hard to see how tensions in the interpretation of the minister's role may arise.

Recent studies of the minister's and the layman's understanding of specific items in ministerial attitude and behavior indicate that there are real differences of other kinds between them.[1] Ministers are inclined to take a professional attitude toward questions of ministerial behavior; laymen, a personal attitude. For instance most ministers feel it is not good practice for a minister to discuss his own family difficulties with members of his parish, while most laymen think it is quite permissible; ministers think that a pastor ought

[1] Milner, "Lay and Clergy Expectations of the Ministry."

not to go on vacation with church families, while lay-men think it is quite all right. Laymen and ministers agree that the pastor has a responsibility to speak out from the pulpit on social issues in the light of Christian gospel; but they sharply differ when matters of local criticism and local demonstrations are in question. Ministers continue to feel that the pastor must be active, while laymen express marked disapproval of such local criticism and activity. At key points the role image of the pastor varies radically in the perception of ministers and laymen because the referent groups defining the role for clergy and laity are different. Hence, a pastor may behave in a fashion which conforms to his understanding of ministerial responsibilities and offend the sensibilities of his lay supporters. Differential role perception is at the root of the misunderstanding here.

Thus far we have indicated that role conflict may involve tensions between two differing roles which a person plays, tension within a single role as a result of role expectations that conflict, and tensions within a single role due to the differences in expectation, as defined by different persons within the constituency of the person who plays the role. There remain the tension possibilities in the fit of the personality of the particular individual playing a role and the role itself. Pastors often deal with emotional collapse occurring when a dependent person is suddenly put in a position which requires him to take an active and independent role. Here is a young man who marries a motherly woman because of deep dependency needs; in effect, he moves out of his parental family into a nuclear family by simply exchanging a dominant mother for a dominant wife. But then his wife becomes pregnant and a son is born to their marriage; at once, this young man is a father, and people turn to him to play the father's role. To be counted upon to care for and nurture the son who is a real competitor with him for his wife's attention and care is often more than such a dependent person can manage; he becomes unaccountably ill, physical symptoms thus protecting him from the demands of the father role. Or he may actually go to pieces mentally and exist for some time in a confused state. His father role and his prior personal organization simply do not fit.

Or take the excellent schoolteacher who is elevated to the principalship of the high school. As a teacher he has succeeded by being sensitive to the reactions of others, ready to guide his conduct by their expressions and needs, and in the work of a teacher such qualities are outstandingly important. Unfortunately they may be related to personal uncertainty and dependence, so that when such a young man is put in a position where he has to make an administrative decision which will displease large segments of his constituency, he finds himself in real trouble. His very sensitivity to others makes any decision which will hurt other people an agony for him; so he procrastinates, postponing critical choices until the school system drifts into conditions which even he cannot tolerate. His decisions made at that late date are bound to be unfortunate, both in their impact on the school system and in their inner effect upon his life. He is just not constituted in a way to make good in the role of administrator.

No personality is a perfect fit to any role; no role gives complete expression to any personality. A community leader must focus attention on what a particular leadership role requires and what a particular person is capable of doing. To begin with, it is important that we as ministers understand our own personalities in relationship to our work in the church and community. Perfect self-understanding is, of course, impossible, but any one of us can come to grips with his basic needs and typical reactions if he will patiently observe himself in action. We can also study the work of the pastor, both as our parishioners define it and as the general church understands it and note points at which the pastor's role will cause particular difficulties for us. No one does all that is expected of a pastor equally well; indeed, it may well be that the more effective one is in some specialty of ministry the less generally effective he will be.

This matter of specialization poses a real question of church policy. Rural churches often tend to think in terms of a single pastor serving a church or circuit, which means that one man, no matter how specialized his talents, will have to carry on all the activities of the pastor's role. How much more fulfilling to the individual pastor and how much better the service to the church if several ministers, chosen for their complementary talents, constitute a staff to serve a plurality of churches within the community! From the point of view of the minister's personal adjustment, as well as that of the growth of the churches and their members, a staff ministry serving all the churches within the community is appropriate and effective.

What the minister recognizes in himself he should be able to recognize in his administration of the parish: lay leaders are not equally well equipped for every church office responsibility. A rational administration would lead, first of all, to a careful role definition of each of the offices to which laymen are elected. In the light of this analysis the nominating committee is then in a position to present persons for the several offices who will serve in them with a minimum of personal tension and social friction. The man who makes a good trustee may not make an effective and happy church school teacher; a fine teacher may serve with complete ineffectiveness in the office of church treasurer. Let the personality of the nominee and the requirements of the role be seen together before nomination, let alone election, takes place.

Our treatment thus far might seem to indicate that what is significant is a nicety of fit between personal characteristics and role expectations; such a mechanical interpretation is quite false. Some consonance between personal qualities and role demands is essential, but no one is ever effective in playing out a role mechanically. To be really well done, a role must be played with individuality and imagination so that our parishioners know that they can depend upon us but cannot predict with precision what we will do in any given situation. We must learn to distinguish between the essentials of a role and the conventionalities. Many a pastor, for example, is praised by his parishioners with the words: "You'd never think he was a preacher!" What they are indicating is that their pastor does not fit the conventional stereotype of "minister," but that he does carry for them the work of a minister. Thus the pastor has made himself the master of the role and has not allowed the role to dominate him.

In a day of social change, roles change, too. A certain inexactness of fit is essential to survival through change. We mentioned in our first chapter the data supporting the thesis that the better trained the minister is in a classical role the less aware of and adjusted to the community he will be. We must always operate within the ministerial role with a certain tentativeness and openness to new possibilities. The capacity to endure an amount of ambiguity in our role definitions, to delay what might be a premature closure in our interpretation of expectations, is the mark of the mature and the vital pastor.

And in such a day, this also marks the effective lay leader in the church; we must not fence him in with a dated picture of the lay office he holds. It is easy to remember some revered patriarch and feel that the particular office he held must always be carried forward in his terms. But it well may be that the office requires a new and changed interpretation, and we ministers ought to encourage such exploration and reinterpretation among our laymen.

Role conflict is a characteristic of our day; we need to manage it—and help others to manage it—without self-recrimination or projection to others of our own guilt and disappointment when matters do not go right. And similarly our laymen must extend to pastors their support and sympathy as we explore together the new dimensions of the role of the Christian minister.

10

Socialization

We are not born human; that is, personality, as we experience and understand it, is not given at birth; we are born with the potential of humanness. The human infant is helpless at birth, absolutely dependent for survival upon the care provided for him by other human beings. If, by the accident of disaster or neglect, he becomes isolated from more mature members of the human species, he quickly perishes. A few incidents in which children have survived under the care of animals are commonly cited under the title "feral men"; but such cases are extremely rare and seriously questioned. Practically speaking, the survival of the infant organism depends upon its nurture by adult human beings.

This dependence is the beginning of a lifelong process by which others influence our understanding of life and of the nature of our own lives. Adults caring for a human infant do not carry on this nurturing task in a personal vacuum. From their first contacts with the infant they treat him as a human being, superimpose human interpretations upon his mechanical reactions to stimuli, give him love and security by holding him, talking to him, singing to him, patting him, and in the myriad of other ways that love suggests. Almost immediately the child becomes as dependent upon this emotional warmth and care as upon the food and warmth such care provides. Indeed, children who are rejected by their mothers may refuse food and die because of their need for the tokens of human acceptance.

This emotional dependence of the infant on others of his kind is the beginning of the communication process by which he learns from those around him what they expect of him and ultimately who he is. Whenever he behaves in a fashion that his parents or their surrogates regard as unfortunate, they bring pressures of a negative kind upon him by withdrawing or curtailing their positive emotional support. This is no conscious process on their part; confronted by the results of his misbehavior—a milk bottle broken on the floor, for example—they react with the irritation such an incident triggers: voices become strained and harsh, gestures tense rather than yielding and relaxed. These changes in his social environment are deprivations to the baby; he quickly learns to associate them with unwanted conduct and to avoid that conduct. His reward is the maintenance of the emotionally satisfying human environment; thus we have begun to shape his behavior and through that shaping to determine how he thinks of himself. And he reciprocally shapes our reactions to him.

Communication possibilities broaden as soon as the baby begins to vocalize. Parents identify some of his random experimental vocalizations as words and repeat them back to him. Slowly he learns to associate these sounds with relationships which he enjoys; thus, the naming of parents comes among his first words. And his vocalization has an important difference from his other activities; here alone he affects himself in the same fashion that he affects others. Through language self-objectification and self-consciousness become possible; the child not only learns what he is supposed to do, he establishes his identity. This ability to name relationships into which he enters is the beginning of his capacity to accept the various roles expected of him by his social world.

In all of this, the important insight is that the growing infant is principally environed by society; social relations are the first realities he experiences and they set the mental framework within which other kinds of experience are perceived and understood. The little child kicking the chair against which he tumbles is simply reacting to physical reality in terms of the only reality he has experienced, the personal world in which such expressions of exasperation and hostility as kicks have real meaning. Only after a great deal of experience and indoctrination is he able to make the necessary abstraction implied in the concept of the material universe.

The relationship of the family to the socializing process is a critical one, so much so that we can say: without the family or some similar nurturing group, the infant organism will not develop its human potential. But the family obviously is not the only socializing instrument; where the family is weak or ineffective, its work will, of necessity, be taken over by other groups. The urban gang has been for at least sixty years a substitute for the family as socializer among the children of foreign or rural migrants to the cities. The slum gang is an index of the pathology of slum families, but not all such pathological families and gangs are in the slums, as the citizens of prosperous suburban communities have frequent cause to discover. Broken or otherwise disturbed families provide so poor a developmental background that the youth gang becomes almost a necessity if children are to remain human. The attempt to use street gangs creatively is a recognition on the part of social leaders of the vital functions such gangs do in fact perform in the lives of their members.

But the family and its surrogates only begin the socializing process; they develop our basic human nature, teaching us what is expected of a human being. The little child learns to face decisions by asking the question, What do my mother and father and brothers and sisters expect of me? Such expectations give him a basis for confident behavior in new and difficult situations, but they obviously do not prepare him for many of the roles which he must play as a full and mature member of his society. Another key group takes over the socialization process at this point, the school. Just as we develop our human nature in the family, so in the school we develop our civic or community nature or learn what it means to be an American.

In speaking of the school we do not refer to the classroom alone but include all the group activities which are organized around the school: the club, the Scouts, 4-H, Hi Y, the teams, school cliques, and all the rest of the manifold social activities of youth. In succession we learn what it is to have a teacher, to be a pupil, to be a member of a class, to be on a team, to be, in fact, a part of our total community. The school begins on material presented to it by the family; when the family has failed, the school finds itself faced with a more difficult job. A teacher reports that children from broken homes take on the average a month longer to get accustomed to classroom routines than do children from normal homes. All of us pay and pay extravagantly for ineffective homes, no matter what the reason for the ineffectiveness.

In the course of the child's passage through school he not only learns the tools of our common trade, so to speak—language, reading, arithmetic, and the like. More importantly, he learns what kind of a person his society expects him to be. Now his question is: What would my teacher, my buddy, my coach, my team, expect me to do? If these expectations are not too different from those he learned in the family, the child shapes his conduct to them with relative ease; but should there exist conflicting expectations, or should the expectations he learns in school seem utterly unrelated to the life he leads, the child will find school a confusing and disturbing experience. Our concern with the "drop-out" is a mark of the seriousness of the problem, for the child who drops out of school is not just refusing to learn his ABCs, he is rejecting our expectations of him. The fact that the rejection may not be a conscious act on his part does not make it any less a real repudiation of the norms of his wider world. Perhaps it would be fairer to him and more accurate in describing the situation not to refer to "*his* wider world" but rather to "*the* wider world" since obviously his inability to internalize the norms the school presents means that its expectations are not his at all.

A third level of socialization is required if truly mature persons are to result: that level is represented by the work of the church. The church builds on what the family and school do, but it pushes beyond them in its norms. Just as we learn to be human in the family and civic- or community-minded in the school, so in the church we discover our divine nature, learn what it is to become members of God's family, strive to enter into the Kingdom of God. These terms are representative of the ideology of Jews and Christians particularly, but similar concepts characterize other religions and their teaching. What the terms say is that we are not really grown up, we have not become what God intended us to be, until we join the church: that is, until we become members of a fellowship which is truly universal. We learn that what we owe to others is not limited by family, or immediate local, or even national community, but involves universal responsibilities across every boundary and barrier.

One of the dogmas of the churches which call themselves "catholic" is framed in the words, "Outside the church there is no salvation." When we make this statement refer exclusively to some single historic fellowship, it must obviously be rejected as unrealistic and imperialistic. But if by "church" we mean a nurturing fellowship that seeks to make us citizens of the universe transcending all parochial bounds, then the dogma is true; men and women do not grow up, they do not realize their full human potential, they are not becoming what God intends them to be until and unless their personalities become socialized in universal terms, in other words, until they join the church. Some may point out with accuracy that many churches are in fact quite provincial and parochial in their outlook and with that observation any sensitive observer must concur. But that does not change the fact that the church is in the world to help men and women grow up, and God intends that the church shall do exactly that.

In what dimensions does the church seek to socialize persons in universal terms? Look at a particular rural church and you will see the dimensions exemplified. On Sunday morning the pastor will read from the Bible and the people will sing from the hymnal. The Bible story he reads is about people in a different land and a different time, people quite unlike the members of the congregation who listen to him. They are Jews and Greeks and Ethiopians and Persians and Romans, and the list might go on endlessly. To all of them so different from us in terms of geography and perspective and so far from us in time we owe an obligation.

On successive pages of one hymnal appear the works of Scotch, American, German, English, Italian, and Polish authors and musicians. The worshiping congregation is celebrating the fact empirically that geography or national origin sets no limits to Christian fellowship and responsibility. People geographically and socially very different from ourselves have contributed to our worship; we cannot permit any social or vicinal separations to divide us from others. Geographic and social space are not meaningful separators among churchmen.

And our reference to Scripture and hymnal above makes clear another dimension in which the church universalizes us. It insists that time does not separate us from others or keep us from having a responsibility to consider them and their welfare in our decisions and activities. Two "time" words characterize religion: tradition and eschatology. They stress the fact that vital religion is never exclusively contemporary, no matter how important it may be to relate religious insight to immediate problems. There is a certain splendid irrelevance about Scripture, hymns, and prayer. They remind us that we are part of a company not sundered by time. To speak of tradition is to stress our responsibility to the persons who preceded us in this earthly life, whose sacrifices have made possible what we now enjoy. But we look ahead as well as backward. There is also in the great religions a lively sense of the future and our responsibilities toward those who will succeed us. The concern of religious persons for conservation and the control of environmental pollution grows out of a proper sense of responsibility to those who will people this world after we are dead. We never live for today only, we are always living out of yesterday and for tomorrow; on this the church must properly insist.

A third concern of the church in the socialization process is to universalize the meaning, the texture of our lives. Jews and Christians, as well as most of the great religions, reject the division of life into "sacred" and "secular"; they insist that all of life is the area for religious commitment and confrontation. We are to act responsibly in all our relationships and not simply in those which are specifically related to church activities. The church teaches us that we may properly neglect its welfare in the interest of the welfare of the community, that there is nothing more sacred in teaching a Sunday school class than there is in sponsoring a 4-H club. Men are not serving God more when they make on offering at church on Sunday morning than they are when they earn the offering in field or shop through the week. Every act of life must be a confession of faith or our faith is no proper faith at all. There are no exclusions from the arena of Christian commitment.

In discussing the socialization process, we have moved beyond the analysis that sociologists make to apply their considerations to the work of the church. What they tell us is that the church, as other agencies and organizations in the community, is constantly at work making its norms real in the lives of its members. What we have added is that this enterprise of the church is part of a team of activities through which human potentials in each of us are brought to their ultimate maturity and fulfillment. Socialization depends not only on conscious planning and rational implementation; it constantly goes on in the communication of attitude and perspective in the total life of a group. The teacher as person is more important to the socializing process than the teacher as technician; the pastor as person is more important in the universalizing function of the church than his preachments or his administration. What he truly is and what he is becoming are the significant data here.

It should require little comment, but we must note the fact of the dependence of church and minister on the prior socializing work of family and school. The church always has an implicit alliance with the family and the school; their failures handicap it and make its socializing task more difficult; their successes become the basis for more efficient and effective operations on its part. We are not suggesting that the work of the family is completely accomplished before the school takes over, nor that the school and family have concluded their tasks when the responsibility of the church begins. In point of time, family, school, and church work together. But the direct impact of the church on us as persons becomes most clear and definite after the earlier work of family and school is begun and well along. Together church, school, and home make growing children of God from the organic potential of infancy. All are needed and are needed together.

11

Culture

All of us constantly use the term "culture" in two
contrasting senses. We refer to a "cultured" person
as one who is cognizant of the niceties and refine-
ments of our social life; his manners are good and he
has a real appreciation of, and concern for, art, literature, the theater and music. We contrast him with the
"uncultured" man, the uninformed and boorish person.
But at the same time we recognize that culture is
something which belongs to everyone, that gentleman
and boor are both a part of our common culture, that
to be "uncultured" in this latter sense is impossible;
without a culture, man ceases to be recognizable as a
human being. It is the latter usage of the term with
which we are concerned as sociologists.

A great anthropologist, Melville J. Herskovits, defined culture in this sense as "the man-made part of our environment." [1] A great sociologist, Howard Becker, began his study of man and his social world, *Man in Reciprocity,* [2] with this definition of culture, "everything that man has made by hand or tongue." He concluded the same volume with this expansion of his earlier words, "what remains of man's past, working on his present, to shape his future."

These men tell us that culture is first of all a uniquely human creation, that it is a significant, perhaps the most significant, part of our environment. We customarily distinguish between material and nonmaterial items of culture, but even material artifacts are not truly parts of culture in isolation from their nonmaterial meanings. The idol that stands on the shelf in a museum is simply a curio to be stared at and admired; its function in the primitive community where it was found was an entirely different and more fearsome one indeed. The difference lies not in the idol or the place but in the meanings that are attached to the primitive figure.

But while culture is a human creation it is not simply a contemporary creation; through it we are tied to the past, to the societies of men who lived before us. All of us in the western world are in a very practical way dependent upon the Phoenecians who, some 3,000 years ago invented the alphabet; all of us when we pay bills or add a column of figures are indebted to the Arabs, and particularly to their sig-

[1] *Man and His Works* (New York: Alfred A. Knopf, 1948).
[2] (New York: Praeger, 1956).

nificant invention of zero and the positional use of numbers. The words we speak and hear, read and write, are communicative devices handed to us through a long history in which their subtle meanings have been distilled. And culture thrusts us forward into the future as well, anticipating our needs by giving us definitions of situations and interpretations of problems which we shall meet. Apparently no other animal form is aware of death as something which will come upon it. But as man I do know death and know that I shall die, a knowledge not given in experience but mediated through our culture. Furthermore, through our elaboration of culture in even small degrees and the process of transmitting it to our children and to their children, we affect the future of men long after our own death has removed us from the human scene.

Culture is a social creation; inventions may be perfected by individuals but they depend heavily upon the social context within which they occur. There are many cases of similar inventions made by independent individuals at almost precisely the same moment; apparently, the basic idea of the invented device occurred to a number of people when a social setting was established in which such a device became feasible and useable.[3] And inventions tend to accumulate as various elements are available, making new combinations and structures possible. Social interaction and consequent social patterns are the stuff out of which

[3] For a discussion of duplicate inventions see Young-Mack, *Sociology and Social Life* (New York: American Heritage Publishing Co., 1962), 2nd ed., pp. 459, 460.

culture grows. Even individual innovation is dependent upon a social context.

From what we have already said it is clear that each of us participates in some particular culture. Most of the readers of this book are Americans and have a common culture as such; it is a culture which stresses the centrality of the individual person as a value in himself, education for all men as a good, upward advancement economically and socially as the norm of personal and occupational behavior, and mobility in the sense of freedom from spatial and mental limits as essential to truly human development. Most of us take these values or norms for granted and may even feel a bit surprised to have them mentioned. Our ethnocentrism has blinded us to the fact that these values are the values of our particular culture growing out of our particular history in our peculiar geographic setting and not universal values of and for men everywhere. Another culture may put the emphasis elsewhere: perhaps it will stress the family rather than the individual as the seat of value; it may consider that education is for children and work for men; it may look with suspicion upon the mobile person, whether his mobility is spatial or social, regarding him as a deserter if he leaves the local group or a suspicious and not-to-be-trusted stranger if he moves in.

With people who differ from us at such central points we cannot help but feel acutely uncomfortable; they indict the values by which we live. Cross-cultural contacts of this kind result in culture shock, a reaction of confusion and uncertainty in the face of the realization of different cultural standards than those to which we are accustomed. Such culture shock, if it can be managed and controlled, is a useful experience in opening the mind to new and innovative possibilities. Such an experience is that of travel seminars studying rural life in western Europe, which confront American seminarians and pastors with a rural life much different from what they know. For instance, in the U.S.A. the proper place for a farmer to live is on his farm (we tend to use the term "suitcase farmer" in a derogatory sense), yet in most European countries the farmer and his family live in town and go out to work in their fields each day; in the U.S.A. we apply scarce manpower to plentiful land, whereas Europeans apply plentiful manpower to scarce land; and again by way of contrast, we are a young nation where new things characterize our thinking, while Europeans live in old communities dominated by a long and meaningful history. When Americans begin to see what they have taken for axiomatic about rural life challenged in their own experience, their minds are opened to new possibilities for their own rural communities.

Culture shock can, however, be a frightening experience, as witness the traveling Americans who express their anxiety by being superficially critical of the European scene, ready to point out how much better things are "at home," and always looking for a "hamburger and coke" to give them gastro-intestinal reassurance. Such persons learn nothing from culture contact; their ethnocentrism is intensified by the experience. Seminars such as the one described above control the negative aspects of culture shock by providing a strong group in which uncertainties and anxieties may be expressed and faced, so that true learning from new situations can take place. Culture shock is potentially present whenever a person from one culture enters a different cultural milieu.

All Americans participate in a common culture, but that is only part of the story. There are subcultures within American culture, and all of us participate in one or more of them as well. All of us belong in varying degrees of intensity to one or another set of hyphenated Americans: Polish-Americans, Greek-Americans, white-Americans, black-Americans—and we might add almost indefinitely to the list. As long as we stay within the confines of our particular cultural enclave, all is well. However, as we have pointed out above, to be an American is to acquiesce in and practice mobility, both spatial and social. When we begin to move about we come in contact with other American subcultures and then we become the potential victims of culture shock. To be a loyal American in a pluralistic society is to be forced into relationships which we find threatening at worst and confusing at best. When black Americans speak of "white racism" they are, among other reactions, giving expression to their own deep experience of culture shock; when they stress "black power" they are reestablishing their personal integrity by reaffirming their subculture. The long drawn-out grape strike at Delano, California, can be understood as two subcultures locked in conflict. Whenever the parties to a social issue are of different ethnic perspective, we may be sure that the issue is colored and clouded by culture conflict and culture shock.

A man who moves from one subculture to another and seeks to make the second his own becomes what sociologists have called "a marginal man." He has left behind his own cultural perspective but is only partially adapted to, and adopted by, the new. There is an element of strangeness in all that he does; he feels unsure of himself because he is unused to the new norms which govern his conduct, thus he stands off on the edge of affairs, alone and lonely. Ministers have many contacts with such persons. They are apt to be more rigid in meeting the standards of their new culture than men native to it are for they are not sufficiently accustomed to the new standards to know which are central and which may be treated with casualness. The city-reared teacher who comes to teach in a rural high school is an example of a marginal man, as is the assistant to the farm adviser who comes to work in central Illinois after growing up in Utah. Such persons need our friendship and acceptance if they are to make the contribution they are capable of making across the gulf separating subcultures.

American rural communities share the national devotion to the values of individualism, education, and mobility, but they do not often sense that this involves them in culture contact and change. When new people in the community are resented and ostracized, or when old settlers are berated for their conservative, dog-in-the-manger tactics, we have examples of culture conflict at work. Sometimes we look at such situations in moral terms and seek to find a sinner or villain who is responsible for all the trouble; we praise and blame when we should understand the situation in terms of differing cultures impinging on one another. We deal with confused and anxious human beings behaving irrationally or immorally on occasion because they feel their essential life style threatened. If we, as leaders, can understand what is happening, we are in a position to be of real help.

Rural pastors themselves, and frequently their wives, are often victims of culture shock. A boy from a working-class home feels a call to the ministry and prepares himself through college and seminary. On graduation he moves to a community which knows him only as the pastor. In that community he moves on a level of equality with men and women in positions of highest leadership. Their subcultural expectations are quite different from those of the humble home from which he came; the differences are bound to create uneasiness if not outright anxiety in the young pastor. A marginal man, he stands between his home atmosphere and the expectations which his new responsibilities lay upon him. The manners which local persons exercise without thinking, he must imitate with conscious care; little that he does can be truly spontaneous since he fears his uncontrolled manners will be inappropriate to his new position. And similar tensions often affect his wife, possibly more than they affect him if she does not have the college education which he possesses.

Many studies have shown that denominational churches have become the accepted social expression of subcultural groups.[4] German immigrants, under necessity of changing their ways in an English-speaking culture, maintained their German autonomy in their Lutheran church. Local tensions between Lutherans and Methodists may have a pseudodoctrinal base but actually be the reflection of cultural distinctness. Whenever pastors in local communities are faced with denominational rivalry and conflict, they should suspect the existence of subcultures in conflict.

Culture contact, culture shock, and culture conflict are implicit in American culture; if we believe in individual achievement, education and mobility, we must expect that people from different cultures and subcultures will be brought together by the simple working of the system. And if our culture guarantees this by its essential nature, then we must be prepared to accept tensions between subcultures, to live with them and to deal with them. Difference need not operate in conflict alone, it may mean enrichment of the cultures in contact. Each of us has something of worth to gain and to contribute to others of differing backgrounds. The work of the town and country pastor is to hold people together in the security of a common fellowship transcending their differences until they can learn of one another and grow together.

[4] H. Richard Niebuhr, *The Social Sources of Denominationalism* (Hamden, Conn.: The Shoe String Press, 1929, rev. ed. 1954).

12

Interaction

Many of us when we think of human behavior almost automatically think of stimulus-response: something impinges upon our perception or consciousness, and we react to it with some more or less appropriate behavior. Originally the stimuli that we can perceive and the responses we can make to them are limited, but the processes of maturation and the associative mechanisms of the conditioned reflex ultimately provide us with an extended repertory of personal reactions. So our thinking goes. We are soon, however, brought to some modification of this simple interpretation, since stimuli themselves are not absolute but subject to conditioning: one and the same stimulus may produce fear in one man and pleasure in another; we are conditioned to perceive stimuli differentially. And even though we may perceive a stimulus in the same way, our responses vary since we vary as human beings. The simple stimulus-response scheme of human behavior must be modified in terms of perception and the uniqueness of the individual person.

A simple stimulus-response explanation is even less satisfactory when we consider interhuman behavior. Here we have, not action and reaction but, constant and intricate interaction. When one man initiates a contact with another, he has some specific exchange of information or service in mind. Suppose he wants simply to inquire the route to some public building in a small town. He stops his car beside the highway and directs his question at a man standing there who stares at him blankly and refuses to respond. The immediate reaction of the inquirer is to regard the nonrespondent's conduct as rude and unfriendly; he may drive away in indignation or he may give vent to his irritation in rough language. He is reacting not just to the other's behavior but to his interpretation of that behavior as well. In effect he says to himself: "If a man asked me for directions and I simply stood and stared at him, I would judge myself to behave in a rude and unfriendly way, and I would deserve to be censured for it." Accordingly, he behaves as if the other man should be censured.

But the other man happens to be a deaf-mute; he stands and stares because he cannot hear and understand. When he senses from the rising color and anger in the driver's expression that the driver is angry with him, he feels helpless and isolated. "What can I do?" he asks himself, "No one understands or accepts me;

I'm all alone." If the inquirer should become aware that his possible informant was a deaf-mute, his whole attitude in the situation would immediately change. From anger at the unresponsive other person he would shift to anger with himself that he had behaved in such an unkind way to a handicapped person.

Here we have illustrated the complexity of human behavior; we may summarize the interactive situation in these terms:

1. Sensing a need for the satisfaction of which I need the cooperation of another person;
2. Perceiving another person who appears to be able to answer the need;
3. As I address him, seeing myself as I think he sees me;
4. As he responds, seeing him as he sees himself in relationship to his perception of me.

And these four steps are only the beginning of the infinitely complex possibilities. In any interhuman situation I am constantly adjusting, not simply to the external situation and the internal need but, to my constantly shifting appraisal of the other with whom I am in relationship as he constantly shifts his appraisal of me.

Interaction is more than conversation, of course; it includes a whole series of social processes directed toward other people. We advance toward them, adjust to them, identify with them, and ultimately develop attitudes of affection and loyalty toward them; or we may turn from them, compete with them, regard them as rivals, seek to injure them, and ultimately seek to destroy them.

In the direction of positive appraisal, interaction moves toward an extreme of complete mutuality— "the two shall be one flesh"—toward the opposite pole we move to extreme antipathy and mortal conflict. Most human behavior reaches neither extreme but moves somewhere in between. Further, relationships between two persons are seldom all of one kind; on the whole we may admire and relate positively to another, but there may be a substratum of animosity and separation which divides us or prevents the development of intense intimacy. Interaction is then a mixing of processes out of which develop the patterned relationships of group life.

When the pastor interacts with his parishioners, an additional factor enters the social field; the pastor is not only an individual person entering into a relationship with another individual, he is also a stereotype in the eyes of the parishioner. This stereotype involves at least two elements: the first includes all the characteristics which a minister is commonly supposed to possess (we think automatically of impracticality, otherworldliness, rigid conventional virtue, weak masculinity, to name a few) ; the second involves the symbolic function of the minister, the fact that he reminds people of holy and mysterious matters, not only in society but in themselves. Thus a parishioner with the stereotype in mind has, at best, an uneasy feeling when he meets his pastor. On the one hand he sees in him a figure which does not command respect, on the other he sees the symbol of his own ultimate loyalties and securities. He cannot patronize the minister without at the same time casting reflections upon his own ultimate commitments; he cannot honor the minister, because he does not appear to be the sort of person who really commands respect.

Many of us sense this uneasiness in the relationship of our people to us; we are now in a position to understand it. It has nothing to do with us as persons; it involves our positions in the community. Our relationships with parishioners and others in the community will improve if we do not feel resentment of their uneasiness with us and if we do not allow their stereotypes to affect us, either in the direction of conformity or of rebellion. As pastors we need to decide explicitly who we are and what our work in the community is; then we need to play it that way, making our position explicit to our parishioners when our behavior seems to puzzle them. Many pastors are unhappy and discouraged because either they are trying to conform to expectations in which they do not believe, or they are acting in ways contrary to those same expectations simply as rebels. Neither conformity nor rebellion is an adequate basis for pastoral conduct.

A recent study indicates that the majority of Methodist laymen in central and southern Illinois feel that the pastor's call should be a friendly, personal chat, while the majority of their pastors feel that the call should be an occasion for serious discussion of religious concerns.[1] In many a small town lay people

[1] Milner, "Lay and Clergy Expectations of the Ministry," p. 95.

are critical of their pastor because his wife does not call with him. Pastors respond to this expectation all too frequently by stating publicly and with a distinctly bellicose air: "You do not pay my wife, you pay me to be your pastor." That statement, though completely true, is as completely irrelevant. Parishioners are looking for a social visit which, in their definition, involves the whole family; pastors see what they are doing as a professional interview and personal ministry.

Suppose a pastor faced this criticism of his wife's failure to call with him frankly and rationally, not resenting the expectation, but countering it with a more adequate one. Let him say something like this: "When I call on you I am always ready to have you talk with me on matters of deepest concern to you, matters which you regard as completely confidential. It's not likely that everytime I call something like that will come up, but if it does I want to be ready for it. If you are going to talk about something of intimate concern to you, it is difficult at best if there are two persons to whom you must speak. In looking from one to the other to see how each is taking your confession, you will be under pressure to hesitate and ultimately to give up the effort to say what you really need to share. If you have only one person to face, you will find it easier to speak. Because I want to make it as easy for you to talk to me as possible, I call alone. However, if a social visit is what you want, invite us over for dinner—we're great eaters." To speak thus is to place the pastoral ministry in its proper context and provide for our people a realistic expectation for pastoral calling.

The symbolic nature of our interaction with others is often less easy to manage because it is less clear. A pastor visits a member of his parish in the hospital and is struck by the man's withdrawn and anxious appearance; he feels unwelcomed by the man and yet senses the man's need for a pastoral ministry. It may be that the problem lies in the pastor's symbolic value to the particular person; many people not too closely related to the church feel that the minister calls on the sick only when their condition is desperate, if not fatal. When the pastor comes, this says in effect to the sick man: "You're on the way out; it's only a matter of days until you'll be dead. They've sent the preacher to see you."

If a pastor suspects that this interpretation is involved in a particular visit, he needs to overcome the symbolic meaning by an explicit emphasis on living and his concern for people in every event and stage of life. A reference to others whom he has visited in the hospital and who are now home well and a discussion of the man's own home and life will frequently overcome the malevolent impression. Whatever tactic we may use to correct misapprehensions, we must constantly remember that, wherever we go, we have a symbolic as well as a personal value to the people who meet us. In an extreme way the pastor is the gospel on the street.

Thus far we have spoken of interaction between two persons; but interaction takes place as well between individuals and groups and between groups.

The process becomes even more intricate when groups are involved, since two processes of interaction, one within the group and the other with the outsider, are going on at the same time. Thus a group may purchase reinforcement and the mutual support of its members by being censorious of and unkind toward persons outside its membership. The rejection of the outsider by the group, often through its leaders, may have the effect of reinforcing group loyalty on the part of marginal members, since the act of rejection shows them how selective and significant the group is.

A case in point might well occur in the relationships of a pastor of a small sect in a county seat town with the ministerial association. Professionally he feels a common bond with the other ministers who constitute the association and would like to work with them, but his relatively weak and unstable church membership provides him a most insecure base from which to work. Other churches in the community have better buildings, finer equipment, more active and diversified programs than his small group can afford or lead. His members, particularly the more prosperous upwardly mobile among them, are constantly tempted to move their participation to one of the other churches. Their children in high school would like to attend youth fellowship groups in other churches with their peers. Under such circumstances it is readily understandable that other ministers represent, through their churches, a real threat to the sect pastor's security. Though he feels drawn as a minister to join with them, as the leader of a small unstable group he also feels the threat of their power. He anticipates that, should he become active in the association and encourage his people to participate in council of churches endeavors, some of them will feel at home with these other churchmen and decide to leave his small group to join one of the larger denominations. A ready and natural response to this threat is to rationalize the differences in theological or behavioral terms. The churches in the council, he informs his people, are not Christian churches at all; they are tainted with apostasy. They do not believe the Bible literally, indeed they carry their disbelief so far that they change "virgin" to "maiden" in their official translations of the Scripture, thus dishonestly altering the Holy Word of God. Further, they are "red" or "pink" at the very least, subversive of those ancient standards that characterize Christian America in its common life. Finally, their members drink alcoholic beverages, are sexually depraved, recommending the legalization of abortion and condoning homosexuality, and gamble at cards and other games of chance. Obviously, he is saying to his people, decent folks like you would not associate with such rascals. "Come out from among them, and be ye separate, saith the Lord, and touch not the unclean thing." (II Corinthians 6:17). External conflict, at the very least the definition of the external situation in conflict terms, purchases internal discipline and loyalty to the group.

To meet such an attack by calling such a pastor a liar and a fraud is to help his tactic work with his people. When pastors attack another pastor, his laymen rally to his support no matter what they may think of him privately. What is being attacked and defended is not the particular pastor but the

pastor as symbol of the particular group. Open reaction to his charges will only confirm his leadership
of the sect. When we understand the interaction between the inner life of the group and the threat of
outsiders, we shall not attempt any defense on rational grounds. Instead, if we are really concerned to
work with this pastor and to help his church, we will
do our best to convert his perception of brother pastors from that of threat to that of support. We will
insist that all the benefits of membership in the ministerial association—participation in services at the
county home and jail, a turn at broadcasting morning
devotions over the local radio, public presence at community-wide services such as high school commence-
ment—be shared with him in rotation; and that all
the advantages of the council of churches program be
available to his church. When he begins to perceive
the other pastors of the community not as rivals but
as allies, his rationalizations will become less necessary and will begin to disappear. It is not even necessary that he change his theological perspective—he
still may feel that his ministerial colleagues are not
simon pure ideologically—but he will be ready to
understand and help them as colleagues even as he
feels understood and helped. He will no longer need
to attack to maintain his leadership in his own
church.

The same interactive situation pertains in other
group relationships within the community. The Farm
Bureau and National Farmers Organization locals
competing for members in the same area will proclaim
highly colored and uncomplimentary pictures of each

other. Political party organizations are expected to be highly critical of one another. Black churchmen calling their white colleagues "white racists" illustrate our point again. The country Methodist church calling the town Methodist church irreligious and immoral, an unfit place for youth to go, is defending its future existence, about which it feels deeply anxious, by attacking the sister church whose strength is seen as a threat. Counter to such negative interactions, larger parish and group ministry movements may be seen as attempts to move churches from a posture of rivalry and threat to a significant perception of mutuality and common strengths.[2]

The concept of social interaction and the processes through which it takes place might well serve as the outline for an entire introduction to sociology. To further complicate our analysis, groups exist within groups. Churches, farm organizations, patriotic and fraternal orders are all parts of a community. If a threat to the total community appears—let us say that a school consolidation plan will close or substantially alter the local schools—the divided churches and other agencies will suddenly unite and present a united opposition to the new plan. How this operates on a national level we may observe in the displacement of rising tides of internal opposition on a foreign enemy.

The moment one person turns to another person or to a group, he has begun to interact with that person or group. Interaction may be either positive or negative and will, in all probability, be mixed. But once we

[2] Judy, *The Cooperative Parish in Nonmetropolitan Areas.*

begin such a process, we are constantly shifting our perspective on the other person or group and on what it is we expect. From moment to moment the pattern of behavior shifts as our understanding of the other and his understanding of us develops and changes. Standing as the other does in his own unique social context, his words and acts may have quite different meanings and intentions for him than they have for us. Our relationship to him will be false and misleading if we are unable at some points in our relationship to see something of the setting from which he speaks and acts. It does no good to bring his statements to the bar of our logic or his acts to the bar of our ethic if these do not agree with the norms to which he is committed. The conclusions we developed in studying communication are advanced, in our study of interaction, from the area of meaning and its sharing to the wider area of behavior and conduct.

13

Status

Like the term "culture," the term "status" is used in two senses: descriptive and normative. Descriptively we use the term to refer to a position within a particular society which has generally recognized responsibilities, authority, privileges, and prestige. Normatively we use the term in relationship to the authority, privileges, and prestige a certain position possesses. When we say: "A doctor has high status," we mean that society generally regards and treats a doctor as an exceptional and privileged person. A minister, a farmer, a truck driver, a housewife, a student—all are statuses in the descriptive sense; and each such status has its place on a normative scale.

Sociologists describe a specific status as being either ascribed or achieved. An ascribed status is one which

an individual possesses by virtue of birth or some
inherent characteristic. It comes to him and he accepts it without any effort on his part; his society
provides it for him. He is expected to occupy that
position, not because of any personal gifts or qualifi-
cation on his part but, solely because he is what he is.
Citizen, schoolboy, and blind man would be examples
of ascribed statuses in American culture. In a traditional society where occupations are hereditary, they
are almost unqualifiedly ascribed statuses.

Achieved statuses, on the other hand, are those
which we earn by our own efforts. In a mobile society
like ours, most statuses are achieved; there are few
jobs to which we are born. Our rulers are not determined by heredity, they are elected; one does not
become a baker or cobbler or carpenter because that
is his family trade; rather, he decides to choose such
an occupation. The characteristic of American society
generally in our day, and of rural society in particular,
is a diminishing number of ascribed statuses and an
increasing number of achieved statuses.

Within a single status there are generally a number
of separate roles and for each role a set of particular
norms. We have previously discussed both role and
norm and have seen that roles and the norms that
support them are social products which we learn
through the process of socialization. In a traditional
society where most statuses are ascribed through
heredity, a member of the society begins to learn the
roles appropriate to the statuses he will occupy as
soon as he is born. For example, the entire intricate
socializing process begins to prepare him for serving

as a farmer; so we speak of farming in such a culture appropriately as "a way of life." But in our society we do not know with any assurance when a child is born what he is to become; hence, the family, in its socializing of the child, prepares him only in very general terms for the roles within the statuses which he is later to occupy. Formal learning must then take the place of informal conditioning in fitting us for the behaviors required in whatever statuses we achieve.

Formal learning, however, while it can prepare us for performing the external behaviors essential to a new status, will not make us feel at home in them, particularly if the norms are other than or contrary to other norms we have accepted from childhood. A certain insecurity, lack of assurance, and awkwardness is bound to intrude into our conduct. Though we may be letter-perfect in our lines, they are still "lines" rather than life for us. We do not feel at home in the parts we are playing; the new status puts us under considerable psychological strain. Only continued successful experience in the status will eventually produce that ease of performance that characterizes one "to the manor born."

In an earlier chapter we discussed the problems of role conflict. It should be evident that there can be no guarantee that within any status the several roles will be consistent with one another. By mentioning only two roles within the status of pastor, those of shepherd and prophet, we can illustrate the possibly sharp conflict resident within the pastor's status. The norms that govern shepherding are tender and accepting; those that govern prophecy are stern, uncompromising,

and judgmental. Yet both roles and their corresponding norms belong to the ministry. Many pastors adjust
by specializing in one role or the other, and perhaps
this adjustment is psychologically the most feasible.
If so, it underlines the importance of staff ministries
as over and against the one-minister-one-church concept for rural Americans. A staff of ministers with
different commitments and skills will provide for parishioners the wide spectrum of service for which people should and do look to their pastor.

Other pastors will feel compelled to attempt within
their own role repertory some adjustment between conflicting roles. They insist that a pastor who carries
out the shepherding role responsibly thereby achieves
a position from which he has more influence in the
prophetic role. People who are sure of their pastor's
love and concern are able to hear his word of judgment
and to accept it for themselves. They may not always
be able to agree with his prophetic evaluations (and
laymen themselves have prophetic responsibilities;
Amos was a herdsman and vinedresser) but they will
give them a hearing, grow in their own appropriation
of righteousness and justice, and thus be encouraged
to develop their own prophetic response. It is obviously
impossible for a finite man to be all things to all men,
but none of us dare escape the challenge of the Pauline
imperative. (I Corinthians 9:22)

A matter to which sociologists give particular attention because of the behavioral tensions produced in
connection with it is status inconsistency. This term
refers to the fact that a particular status may have a
high prestige value at one point and an incongruously

low evaluation at another. It is hard to live with this kind of inconsistency; indeed persons who feel the pinch of status inconsistency are tempted to regard their society as unjust and other persons as insincere and hypocritical. A black physician may find attitudes and expressions of appreciation, respect, and honor in his work in the hospital or clinic where he practices; there he has prestige and influence. But when he leaves the clinic he becomes a black man unable to rent or buy a house in certain parts of town, unwelcomed by certain social clubs, often tragically unwelcome in our churches. The incongruity between the treatment he receives as physician and as a black may lead him to regard cynically the ideals of American society and to be very sceptical about any admiration expressed to him by white associates. It may also result in an element of tentativeness and uncertainty in his behavior, since he can never be quite sure of his position or acceptability in any particular situation.

The minister suffers from status inconsistency as well. On the one hand his position in the local community prestige structure is universally high. In our earlier discussion of community power structure we discussed the differential prestige rankings accorded different occupations: all such studies give the minister or clergyman a relatively high ranking.[1] George Counts' 1933 study ranked the minister fourth in prestige of forty-five occupations exceeded only by bankers, college professors, and physicians in that order. National Opinion Research Center studies placed the min-

[1] See detailed discussion in Taylor, *Occupational Sociology*, pp. 169-70.

ister with psychologist, mayor of a large city, and member of board of directors of large corporation thirteen in ninety in 1947 and tied for 17.5 out of ninety in 1963. His score in both years stood at eighty-seven with a high of ninety-six, low of thirty-three and average of seventy for all occupations in 1947, and a high of ninety-four, low of thirty-four and average of seventy-one for all occupations in 1963.

The minister's prestige is relatively high in his community not because of his personal gifts or achievements but because of his ascribed status. That status, however, is declining, relative to other professions and occupations. In 1968 of one hundred fifty-six members of the Rural Sociological Society who expressed an opinion as to whether the status of the rural minister was rising or falling, fifty-four percent felt his status was falling, twenty-four percent said it was rising, and twenty-two percent indicated it remained stable. The evidence is that ministers, though still accorded much prestige, are not in as elevated a position as they once held.[2]

Students in Professor Clinton L. Folse's class in rural sociology at the University of Illinois in the winter of 1968 spent some time in discussing with the author the reasons for this apparent decline in ministerial prestige. From the discussion emerged five observations:

1. The businessman has risen in prestige. (This may be true in the rural communities from which

[2] Smith et al., *The Role of Rural Social Science in Theological Education*, p. 36.

these students come, but is not indicated in the national polls referred to above.)

2. The decay of faith in God has affected the status of the clergy.

3. The ministerial profession has declined in the quality of men who enter it. (This does not explain the decline of an ascribed status except marginally; apparently the students were thinking of the fact that pulpits formerly occupied by full-time trained pastors may now be served by students.)

4. The general level of education has gone up, so that the minister no longer is the only or one of the few educated men in the community.

5. The church, which fifty years ago presented virtually the only opportunity for socialization which most rural people possessed, has now been supplemented by many social institutions and agencies which are in fact competitors; since the church is less necessary to local people, its leaders are less important.

Pastors will wish to examine these observations in detail as they apply to their own situations; to the extent that any or all of the observations are true in a given community, they will contribute to the uncertainty of the pastor. Older pastors, particularly, accustomed to a certain level of acceptance and honor, may feel depressed because they see occupations formerly less highly considered now given priority over the ministry. A natural tendency when we observe such a development is to feel that we are failing personally. No such conclusion is justified from these facts. It is not the individual minister who is marked down here, it is the ascribed status of clergyman. If the status we hold as minister declines in prestige, that occurrence affects us personally, but we are not personally responsible for the decline, which is a social appraisal of the ministerial status in relationship to other statuses and not a social judgment on the man in the office.[3]

The relative status of the minister is an important factor in our administration of the minister's office, but it is not status inconsistency: what we are concerned about in that matter is the tension between a high prestige accorded to our office and a relatively low appraisal of the office indicated in other ways. The tension is illustrated in data from a study of Illinois Methodist pastors and laymen in the central and southern parts of the state.[4] Ministers and laymen were asked to express their agreement or disagreement with a number of statements. One statement was: "Ministers are among the most influential leaders in any community"; seventy-four percent of the laymen agreed with this statement, but only fifty-three percent of the ministers. Another statement was: "Most ministers are underpaid for what they do"; here the proportions of agreement were almost exactly reversed, with only fifty-three percent of the laymen agreeing that the minister is underpaid, while seventy

[3] For a helpful discussion of this whole issue see James D. Glasse, *Profession: Minister* (Nashville: Abingdon Press, 1968).
[4] Milner, "Lay and Clergy Expectations of the Ministry," pp. 78, 79.

percent of the ministers agreed with the statement. Here status inconsistency is disclosed by the data. Ministers feel that there is a real discrepancy between the influence they are supposed to possess and the financial remuneration they in fact receive; on the one hand they are treated as the equals or superiors of everyone in the community and on the other they are paid at a level well down toward the average of the community or below. They cannot help but sense something phony about the prestige accorded them and something essentially insincere about laymen who talk one standard of appreciation and pay another.

Further, they face real behavioral difficulties because of this dual evaluation of ministerial status. To occupy a position of community prestige involves one in certain patterns of conduct. One must possess the appurtenances of culture in his home, his children must take music lessons, go to camp, belong to the scouts, attend college: all of these activities cost money, a cost which the pastor finds difficult to meet in a period of escalating inflation. Pastor and wife face real problems as they try to maintain their position on the income available to them; the number of pastors' wives teaching school to extend their husbands' income is an index of the severity of the problem.

And this is but one illustration of the tensions implicit in status inconsistency. Samuel W. Blizzard [5] has documented others. For example, rural pastors in a panel he studied devoted on the average thirty-four minutes a day to sermon preparation and one hour

[5] "The Minister's Dilemma," *The Christian Century,* April 25, 1956.

and four minutes a day to stenographic tasks. It is not difficult to imagine what this does for ministerial morale. The December 1968 issue of *Ministry Studies* is given over entirely to a discussion of "Role Conflict Among the Clergy." Edgar W. Mills, who edited the issue, defines the task of parish leadership in a modern church as "the entreprenurial direction of a voluntary association" and points out that this task and the model of ministry presented in the modern seminary are essentially unrelated. Thus the seminaries build into their graduates an element of status inconsistency.

In the Spring 1969 issue of the *International Educational and Cultural Exchange,* Homer Higbee, in an article entitled "Role Shock—a New Concept," deals with a similar problem occurring when a professional man leaves his own country to become a student in the U.S.A.[6] He discusses cases of such men dropping out of a graduate program of study to return home before the completion of their work, and his accounts sound very much like case studies of men dropping out of the pastorate. This writer, for example, left a full-time pastorate to become a graduate student and can give personal testimony of the uneasiness which affected him as he moved from filling a secure position of responsibility and regard in a community to the relative anonymity and normlessness of student status at a great university.

Another tension which pastors feel is that between the respect accorded them in public affairs and their apparent powerlessness to bring about significant

[6] Pp. 71-81.

changes in public life. Young pastors who envision a better world become disturbed and discouraged when they seem unable to get even a hearing for their proposals of change in the seats of authority. Part of their difficulty we have already discussed in pointing out the need of understanding the decision-making process and how it may be influenced. But there is still an inner sense of powerlessness which the pastor often feels. It will help him if he realizes the nature and scope of the power he does in effect wield. Jeffrey K. Hadden in the final chapter of his study, *The Gathering Storm in the Churches,*[7] gives a particularly perceptive treatment of the pastor's power base.

Hadden's point is that if the clergy are to counsel meaningfully with laymen, they must be better informed than they now are in the theological issues of the times and be more cognizant of the facts of a given social situation or problem. Laymen do not respect enthusiastic ignorance. With that conclusion we all must agree. But there is an additional consideration we must honor if we are to exercise the power that does in fact belong to us as pastors. No one respects the advice of a man who demonstrates that he does not know enough to do his own job well. Only as laymen become convinced that a pastor is a competent professional in his own field will they listen to his observations as to how they should conduct themselves in politics or economic life. If the traditional work of the ministry is not carried on with skill and sensitivity, we can get little hearing for other aspects of our task; but if our laymen

[7] (Garden City, N. Y.: Doubleday and Co., 1969), p. 209 ff.

hear thoughtful, well-argued sermons, participate in services in which, because of our competent preparation, they are enabled to worship, and if when they are in trouble they find a sympathetic and helpful pastor ready and willing to meet them, then they will respect him in his social and civic roles as well. The power stance of the pastor rests in the pastorate effectively conducted, and no amount of social technique will help him who is not faithful and skillful in this basic task.

In a sense, all our previous concepts have found unity and summation in our consideration of status. A status is defined for us by culture and given to us through the process of socialization; it comes to expression in interaction within the community; within each status are a number of roles and for each role a set of definitive norms; understanding our particular statuses and the roles and norms associated with them not only as we see them but as they are defined by others around us enables us to communicate with those others in essentially meaningful fashion; each status we occupy has a position in the community power-structure and plays its part in the community decision-making process. Thus what we have been dealing with in defining and analyzing ten concepts, regarded by rural sociologists as of major importance for the work of the rural pastor, is not ten separate realities but ten elements within the single ongoing reality of our common life. Their unity is given not simply in logic but in the more meaningful unity of the lives we live together.

14

The Case of the Missing Concept

The ten concepts dealt with successively from chapter 4 through chapter 13 were chosen by members of the Rural Sociological Society as "of major importance" for a pastor serving a town and country church. These ten were their top choices from a list of forty-nine concepts compiled from recent textbooks and the last five volumes of *Rural Sociology,* the professional journal of the society. Among concepts they passed by in favor of the ten were such familiars as "locality group," "Gemeinschaft-Gesellschaft," "ecology," "stereotype," and "trade center," as well as such economic concepts as "family farm," "market economy," "elasticity of demand," and "land tenure."

The sociologists were invited to add to the list any additional concepts they might consider important.

Few did in fact write in any concepts, but among those written in were "marginal man," "ethnic group," "urban," "social change," "social action analysis," "authority," "power," "charisma," "social systems," and "boundary maintenance." Except for "social change" listed by three persons each of these concepts was written in only once. We mention them here only to indicate the wide variety of concepts available to and used by the sociologist in studying the rural scene.

Perhaps our readers have noted already one very significant omission from the list: why, in a day when "confrontation" is the word and mood of the hour, did no one, either in the literature or on the questionnaires, mention the concept of "social conflict" as one "of major importance" to the work of the town and country pastor? A generally recognized technique of social action is to promote conflict within a community between some category of underprivileged and the "establishment." The occasion of conflict need not be important or the facts adduced true; what is important is that the experience of challenging authority will unite the underprivileged into an active group. Becoming a group gives the powerless power. So central is this practice of conflict inducement as a device for social change in the contemporary social scene that we should give thought to its omission from the sociologists' thinking.

To begin with, we ought to note that the sociologists did make room for the fact of social conflict in the concepts they chose as important. "Social interaction" was a concept which fifty-five percent classified as "of major importance" and, as our earlier discussion indicated, social interaction includes a number of processes, among them that of conflict. We need to learn from practitioners in the field of social science that conflict is not something independent of other phenomena, but exists as a social process dependent on other social processes, taking its real meaning from its social context. *Social* conflict involves prior community interaction and is meaningful for society only as long as that community continues and is enhanced. Conflict that disrupts and makes community ultimately impossible ends by destroying the parties to the conflict; society indeed contains conflicting forces, but the adhesive forces must predominate or society ceases to exist and anarchy prevails.

Secondly, I think it true—though this represents a conclusion not from data but from my own experience—that sociologists in general feel unhappy about social conflict and therefore tend to give it negative value. They know it well, for their studies frequently bring them in contact with it, and they observe its basically destructive character. They have seen conflict over school consolidation divide the already limited economic resources of a town and country community, dissipate needed funds in unnecessary building projects, fixate fundamentally untenable school district structures around the quickly constructed new buildings, and leave generations of children to suffer from an inadequate education. They have watched zealous pastors divide the citizenry over issues that were central and significant in the sixteenth or the nineteenth centuries but which have nothing to support them but words in the twentieth century, and they know that these issues are merely rationalizations of social differences which the ministers do not recognize and would be ashamed of if they did. The sensitive pastor has only to reread Richard Niebuhr's *Social Sources of Denominationalism* to become aware of how religious rationalizations can clothe social differences. When we experience something as destructive as social conflict, it is human to ignore its influence when and if we can.

But the pastor dare not forget the fact of social conflict, and he must confront it with two questions:

1. What are the social situations out of which conflict emerges? and
2. How can such conflict be managed for the good of persons and the community without which they cannot exist?

We shall attempt to answer the questions in that order.

There are two sets of external, or objective, factors which lead to conflict between persons and between groups: scarcity of an item which both parties want or need, and inequitable distribution of the wealth produced by common efforts of both parties. The first situation may be as simple as one apple and two boys or one television set and a divided opinion as to which program we wish to view; or it may be as complex as the rivalries of oil companies and their supporting nations for oil drilling rights in the Middle East. The first type of situation may be seen in a town and country community with a declining population base when a new teacher is employed by the public school system and is subsequently visited in succession by the pastors of the several local churches in their hope of securing, each for his particular church, this scarce and valuable human resource. The second situation holds when union and management negotiate, under threat of a strike or lockout, for wage-scales and profit-sharing arrangements whereby a larger share of the common product is allocated to the one or the other. It may also be observed when the older members of the church are providing funds for the refurbishing of the cemetery while the youth are pressing for scholarship funds for youth camp.

The two situations require different types of treatment and one of the first necessities in resolving such conflict is to determine which of the two situations we face. If the basic issue is scarcity, then we may choose between expanding the supply or curtailing the demand: applied literally in the case of the churches competing for a new teacher this would mean increasing the local population or decreasing the number of churches. Neither of these alternatives is very realistic, but at least we are aware of objective limitations and do not blindly compete against one another. If there are no local industries which may employ additional population, then we must perforce settle for a limited population base and either reduced church programs or churches working together in some form of federated effort.

If the situation is one of competition over the sharing of a common product, then we must set up some pattern of priorities on which both parties in conflict can agree. What is it that both young and old church members mentioned above are concerned to put first? Can they not agree that the proclamation of the good news of Jesus and his revelation of God's outgoing love to men everywhere is the one function above all others that the church must undergird? If that is the central priority of the church, then cemeteries and youth camps fall into appropriate focus. If youth camp is only a recreational experience for the insiders in youth group leadership, then we cannot press its claims too sharply; but if youth camp means extending the gospel to youth by training our active youth for mission and enlisting our marginal youth in participation, then the youth camp's priority is high.

On the other hand, if our desire to adorn the cemetery is for purposes of prestige and pride, we cannot rate the expenditure of material resources to that end as having high priority. Yet the care of and for persons is a Christian obligation, and we owe a debt of concern to the dead as well as to the living; indeed, persons who have little respect for their dead show a declining concern for the living. Hence, it well may be that a Christian concern for the care of the cemetery would come high on our priority list. Knowing exactly what it is we are trying to do as a church helps us to ask the discerning questions about both projects and then to find a reconciliation in our conflict.

Incidentally, such exploration might very possibly reveal the resources to carry out both projects. Cemetery care is largely a matter of physical work, work that youth can do with great enthusiasm and enjoyment; if our youth are led to care for the cemetery, then obviously funds earmarked for it can be used for youth camp scholarships. There is no guarantee that a determination of priorities will enable us to get what both sides wish in the conflict. Sometimes wishes are mutually incompatible, but surprisingly often we can get more through such discussion and consequent action than we originally deemed possible.

As technology helps us to make a more adequate use of our material resources, economic scarcity will become less a factor in producing conflict so that external situations of this first type will less frequently exist to cause conflict. However, experience indicates that resources may be substantially expanded without reducing conflict, for expectations constantly expand of what is minimally satisfying. Oldsters who remember the depression of the 1930s will define poverty in quite different terms than do children of the affluent sixties. Deprivation is always relative and not dependent simply upon objective criteria of nutrition, shelter, and medical care; it always has to be understood in terms of what persons in a particular society think they need to live on to maintain a minimal level of decency. In our society a family without color television may feel deprived; in old China a family without resources to provide a proper and ostentatious funeral for a family member felt itself deprived. Social definitions of what items are essential to the good life differ between societies and change within a society.

However, even though technological plenty might indeed provide an adequate and a satisfying level of living for all, there will still be objective conflicts of the second type: those growing out of differences as to how the common social product shall be shared. We must be prepared for fundamental and long-term conflict growing out of such differences, even when the subject of our differences is a matter of prestige or authority. Black power, student power, youth power, and woman power conflicts have to do with the sharing of decision-making authority within society, and these conflicts will be with us for a long time. We must be prepared to deal with them.

Internal factors provide us with a basically different type of conflict situation. Here the conflict is induced by inner necessity rather than outer reality. I pick a fight with someone because I feel frustrated, irritated, and angry; the fact that the man I am angry with is not the cause of my emotional state and can do nothing about it does not prevent me from spewing out my anger upon him. The discharge of my anger is a means of reestablishing my own dignity and sense of worth. Similarly, groups become involved in conflict to maintain and increase group solidarity. Group members who have come to question the leadership of their group may often renew their support for the leadership enthusiastically when their irritation becomes redirected against another group interpreted as threatening their own. Inner unity is frequently purchased at the price of outer conflict: experienced pastors in town and country communities know how often weak groups use this device to stay alive and active. Community disruption is the price such groups are willing to pay for group survival.

Negotiation as to priorities or other factors in the external situation is relatively useless if social conflict is of this type, and any approach which seems to smack of opposition or correction will only aggravate the tensions. Persons who feel threatened personally or in their group life will regard any opposition as further threat; in some way taking the pressure of insecurity off such persons is the only action which will help resolve the conflict their needs have defined. Anything which can give such persons and the group with which they are associated public recognition will to that extent make the conflict they are raising less necessary to them. It is never enough to accept their definition of the causes of conflict as the subject of negotiation; what is really being negotiated is human dignity and group strength.

What is the pastor faced with conflict in his community to do, how is conflict to be managed? First of all, conflict is to be recognized openly; any disposition to gloss over rifts and differences will not produce a united community but, to the contrary, an even more divided one. What is kept secret or hidden gains the power associated with mysterious and forbidden things; it will very likely even escalate the conflict, since people will be facing essentially unknown opposition. We should expect conflict to exist in a growing society, be on the lookout for its manifestations, and be ready to deal with them.[1]

In this matter of being alert to conflict, it is important that a forum be available for conflicting views and opinions in the community structure; in many

[1] An excellent discussion is found in Lyle Schaller, *Community Organization: Conflict and Reconciliation* (Nashville: Abingdon Press, 1966).

rural communities all that dissidents can do is rebel. There is no place to which they may take their complaints and suggestions. Church-wise, an active ministerial association involving all the ministers, both professional and lay, in the community is the absolute minimum. To its membership individual persons should be invited as ministers and not as representatives of their churches: the professional bond is sometimes adequate to unite us when ideological differences and ethical perspectives are quite alien. If a community council of churches is possible, that is even better; laymen should represent their churches and hold the key offices. And for the community as a whole in its total organizational life, there should be a representative community council to which all groups within the community would be expected to send delegates. With this social machinery the community is in a position to anticipate conflicts, to hear dissident parties, to reach out through community programs to meet the objective needs, and to provide a forum in which internal needs can find a hearing and an expression. It is suggestive and significant that the term "community organization" has been chosen to refer to the effort to organize segments of the community for conflict purposes; such procedure is about all that is left if the community does not provide an organization in which the needs of the citizens may be expressed and through which they may work toward the solution of community problems.

Important as it is to get people to talk to one another in a conflict situation, it is even more important to get them to do something together. Community activities which cut across the conventional lines of separation enable persons of different backgrounds to know one another and to establish trust in one another as human beings. Such procedure, not practical in mass societies with their impersonalism, is a resource which we in the town and country community have. We ought to make use of it to transcend the differences that produce conflict.

A second important step is to determine whether the issues in the conflict are largely external or internal; almost always we shall find a mixed situation, but it is possible to sense whether the external adjustments are the important focus or whether the assertion of personal integrity and group stability is chiefly in view. A clarification of these issues will indicate what procedures will be promising in effecting reconciliation. On the contrary, failure to discriminate between the two types of conflict will lead to frustration, both on the part of the conflicting parties and also on the part of the agents attempting reconciliation.

Openness to the expression of conflict, community and church structures which can provide forums for conflicting perspectives, dialogue and common action between parties to the conflict, and diagnosis as to the type of conflict we face are all essential if community solidarity is to be achieved and maintained. When conflict suggests the importance of innovative social change, then the pattern of community decision-making which we have previously suggested is important. Something new in the community is very frequently the appropriate reaction to social conflict.

Before we conclude, it is important to suggest some

of the positive possibilities in social conflict, for if we fail to see what conflict is accomplishing, we may fail the community we are striving to preserve. Conflict often discloses to the total community unmet needs of large categories of citizens. Unserved persons may suffer from hidden hungers which conflict alone brings to our general attention. None of us likes to look at ugly things, particularly ugly things within the community which we enjoy and of which we are proud. But anyone who truly loves his community wants it to become more responsive to the human needs of all its people. When conflict comes it often calls our attention to need, and this is a most important contribution to the community of the future.

Through conflict, troubled persons are often able to express their inner frustrations in a socially acceptable way. Our society with its technology has, in a sense, hemmed us all in; it becomes more and more difficult to express our resentments and our resistances. We are spun around in the technological whirl and come to feel that we have no independence or freedom or integrity. Feeling this way, we must break out and express ourselves somehow for the sake of our personhood. Many quarrels and conflicts within the church, for instance, arise because people need to give vent to deeply felt hostilities in a social atmosphere where they can feel accepted. We should encourage such expressions of conflict as a healthy procedure in a mass society.

Conflict may lead persons to a new sense of dignity and worth; they may learn that they do not have to come hat-in-hand to the power figures of the community, but that they have the power to carry on autonomously. In the early history of industrial development in England and America, the cooperative movement gave to ordinary people a sense of being in control of their own destinies. Unions for the mass industries in the mid-thirties served the same function; workers felt a pride in their position and confidence in what they could do through their newly established unions. Such pride in self, such independence, are more important products of cooperatives and unions than their economic benefits, important as those may be.

Finally, conflict may serve as the basis for uniting a number of separate persons with a common problem into a working group. This is the philosophy that motivates the "community organization" movement. There is no easy guarantee that it will work, but there is a possibility that a new social cohesion will develop among persons who come together to fight in a common cause. How to make this cohesion endure beyond the incidents and conflicts that originally inspired it is a constant problem of the community organizer. On the one hand he wants to make the conflict a means of getting to the conference table with the power-holders of his community, yet he knows that in beginning to negotiate he may lose his position of strength because his supporters will lose interest when the conflict is muted. None of us has a satisfactory solution to that dilemma; each of us works out a particular solution in each different situation. There remains the real possibility that out of conflict may come a new, vital participation in the life of the community.

Conflict is a constant element of the social context;

with such change as we now seem fated to experience, there will be much more occasion for conflict
in the future than in the past. No rural pastor can
avoid it or should try to; what he should try to do
is to understand the conflicts he meets and deal with
them openly, knowingly, and courageously.

15

The Learning Church

We began with the thesis that a sociologically sophisticated pastor makes for an effective church; the church and its redeeming work in the town and country community are the focus of all we have said thus far. We have been addressing ourselves very largely to the pastor, whose responsibility it is to direct the work of the church. Yet the pastor is not the church; indeed, he is often only an itinerant, leading a particular local church for a limited period of time. What the church really accomplishes is determined by its laity and their long-term effort to understand the community within which they function and to serve that community in the light of their church responsibilities. We should now inquire how the pastor may best help

these laymen and laywomen to appropriate the social
science insights we have been discussing.

Nothing is learned simply by being told about it.
You will recall our earlier account of the experience
of the young pastor in Iowa who made an eloquent
presentation to his church board on the need for new
and expanded Christian education facilities. Board
members listened with polite attention to all he had
to say, yet obviously were not moved. Six months later,
however, they were ready to proceed in building and
paying for the property he had recommended. In the
interval the plan had become their own. Only when
the data which the pastor had collected and presented
was thoroughly appropriated by the congregation over
a period of time did it possess any motivational power.
Facts are never enough; they must always be facts
which people are able to relate to their own situations.

Once we appreciate the central significance of self-
discovery, we shall find many sources of data through
which a pastor may lead his people in understanding
their church and community. Some of these are historical: prior pastors and committees may have made
church and community reports which lie somewhere
unused in the church files. When a minister enters a
new pastorate his first search should be for such
earlier studies. Inadequate though they may prove to
be by contemporary standards they will provide a
bench mark against which to see the current status
of the church and its local world. The search should
not be limited to the files of the local church; district,
presbytery, synod, conference and area offices often
have surveys which cast light on the local church. The

state council of churches may have relevant files, particularly in situations where some program of interchurch cooperation has been attempted or developed. An interested pastor will ally himself with his laymen in exploring all possible reservoirs of data from the past.

And such reservoirs are not limited to ecclesiastical files; in the local community there are often excellent surveys which have been conducted by the school board or the chamber of commerce. Educators and businessmen in the laity of the church should be asked for help in unearthing such forgotten resources. The very search for such previous studies serves to alert local leaders to the possibilities of studying their own situation, even though they may not discover that much has been done in the past. The fact that the pastor thinks it possible that studies have been made and asks for help in locating them is the beginning of motivation for a current study.

There is also the possibility that the state experiment station and the state extension service have made studies which impinge upon the local community. Inquiry regarding this is best addressed to the farm adviser in the county where the pastor serves. Should he be uninformed or unable to help, a letter or visit may be directed to the rural sociology department in the agricultural college of the state. Its quite possible that no pertinent studies have been made, but the pastor needs to know that before he begins any new study, and his inquiries will gain him the interest and support of a number of people in the local community and in the county and state.

Incidentally, there is infrequent and poor cooperation and coordination of research among the several professional agencies at work in the field. A case in point is a study just published by one of the great state universities in which the authors have surveyed and analyzed a rural area within which a large industrial complex is in process of establishment. The study is well done, but apparently its authors are completely ignorant of a prior study carried on by an ecclesiastical research agency two years earlier. The studies overlap and the more recent could have profited by knowledge of the former. Any student should begin his analysis of a local problem by looking to see what has been done or not done with the same problem by others earlier.[1]

Suppose that the pastor does discover one or more earlier studies of his particular church and community; at once he needs help in interpreting them, help that can be given effectively only by local people. He can turn both to official committees and boards of the church and to individual leaders for the help he needs. As he talks with them, certain evaluations of prior studies will begin to emerge, and this sets the stage for the significant question: "What is the situation now?" Thus the pastor will begin to mobilize interest in, and motivation for, a current up-dating of

[1] Gene F. Summers, Richard L. Hough, John T. Scott, C. L. Folse, *Before Industrialization: A Rural Social System Base Study* (Bulletin 736, Urbana, Illinois: University of Illinois Agricultural Experiment Station, December, 1969); and Douglas W. Johnson, *Upper Illinois Valley Planning Report* (Evanston, Illinois: Bureau of Social and Religious Research, September, 1967).

prior surveys or a completely new effort. It is worth taking time to interest people generally so that a substantial number of citizens with varying talents and diverse points of view may be enlisted in the eventual study, not by pastoral invitation or draft, but on their own initiatives.

In the Fall 1969 issue of *Review of Religious Research,* John Niles Bartholomew has presented an evaluation of three different approaches to local church and community studies developed by the Board of National Missions of the United Presbyterian Church in the United States of America: (1) survey by an outside expert, (2) self-study, and (3) "Exploration of Mission," a scheme to get local persons to study their church and community out of a theological understanding of the meaning of the church and its message.[2] In general his conclusions are:

1. The results of the survey by an outside expert were most accurate and predictions of trends were largely supported by ultimate developments, but the local churches made very little, if any, use of the recommendations of the experts.
2. Self-study produced relatively accurate appraisals of the ecological patterns, but often frightened local people because they saw dangers for their churches but no way out; they tended, on this basis, to decide in favor of actions and programs geared almost exclusively to institutional survival.
3. Results of the "Exploration of Mission" technique were varied, related to the initiative of local

[2] "A Study of Planning Techniques for Local Congregations," pp. 61-65.

churchmen in developing the project, the enthusiasm of the pastor for it, and the development of small working committees in place of large ones; but the most significant factor associated with a church and community study conducted in this way was the fidelity of the members of the study committees to the Bible study aspect of the program. Where committees took Bible study seriously, they were able to look beyond institutional survival to the work which the church must do in its local community.

This careful analysis suggests that a survey will have real impact upon church programs when it is carried out by local people with the counsel or guidance of experts, undertaken for the sake of the gospel and its increased effectiveness in the local community. Such a study should not be seen as the special project of a new pastor or a gimmick to help the church keep going, but rather as the utilization of modern skills and knowledge to enable the church to carry out with greater effectiveness its age-old responsibilities. It should grow out of the unique life and work of the church and not be superimposed upon it. We might summarize the survey process as involving an intricate interaction between faith, facts, and fellowship. In terms of our faith we ascertain and evaluate the facts in the strength of the fellowship.

The several denominations and many state councils of churches have research experts who can and will provide self-study guides and often give personal assistance in outlining subject matter and procedure in carrying out a church and community survey. Correspondence with the appropriate denominational official and the office of the state council of churches will determine what is available in published form and what expert help can be secured. Often college sociology departments or the research bureaus at theological seminaries are ready to help. There is a whole series of agencies whose resources are available to the pastor and his church in making an objective study of their setting.

When they are contemplating a survey, both pastor and people should consider whether they cannot enlist support for the effort from other churches in the community. A united approach to fact-gathering ensures a more willing response on the part of those to whom we go for information. Outreach to other churches for a community-wide effort may slow down the timetable of the survey, but it is often worthwhile to get better and more useable data even though we must delay a bit in securing it. And there is no reason why we should not make alliance with nonchurch agencies within the community in such a survey as we plan. The high school social science teacher and his classes may be eager to help; and the local business and professional men's association as well as trade union and farmer organizations are often willing to work on a community-wide study.

Below I shall outline what I consider to be the appropriate elements in such a survey, but I must begin with the warning that what is immediately vital is to find answers to the questions which people in the church and community are already raising. It may be argued that they are asking the wrong questions, but that is a matter of professional opinion. They will never be brought to what some of us believe are the right questions until the pressing matters that trouble them are dealt with. Therefore any survey should begin by listing as broadly as possible the matters about which the people involved want information. After these are listed we can list opposite each question the sort of data that would provide an answer and the source from which we expect to discover such data. In the course of making the list, new and related questions will appear, and we shall be ready to see the community as a whole. But that wholeness of view should be the end of the process and not its beginning.

With that proviso, let us see what elements are appropriate to a church and community survey. Perhaps foremost in our minds is the matter of geography: just what area of farmland and village we are responsible for as pastors and as people. We have dealt with various theories in the ecology of community in our previous discussion of the community concept. Here we stress that any church survey will want to get the church in focus as it relates to the significant geographic limits of its people.

The people themselves constitute the second survey element; actually they are primary, but we are scarcely in a position to deal with this aspect of the survey until we know the area within which our responsibility lies. Just the number of people and how that number has increased or decreased over the years are important data. The relative proportion of different categories of persons within that number should be considered next: Are men or women numerically in the ascendancy? What is the relative proportion of persons in the several age categories? What about marital status and the interrelationship of marital status with age and sex? Are there many unmarried adults and are they originally single, widowed, divorced, or simply separated, either by accident or by intention? What about the ethnic backgrounds of community members? Are there numbers of the so-called "minority groups" —blacks, Indians, Spanish-Americans? The list of such questions could be extended almost endlessly.

A third survey element is socio-economic: What are the wealth and the income of the members of the community? By wealth we refer to basic resources, such as land, minerals, and industry. By income we refer to the economic product of those basic resources and its differential distribution among the populace. Just as we referred to geographic areas as the significant limits for our definition of population, so we must refer back to our survey of the populace in assessing the meaning of socio-economic wealth and income. Are any of the population categories discriminated against in the distribution of the community's resources? How adequate is this among different categories?

This latter question brings us to the fourth element in a community survey, the several services available to people in a particular community. These services will depend in large measure upon the wealth and income of the community. A poor community will not be able to afford a bank and, lacking a bank, the people will not be able to secure the credit they need or will secure it at a disadvantageously high cost. The degree of affluence will also set limits on the health services a community can support; hospitals and doctors are expensive. As we explore the services of our community we shall be investigating facts which comment upon our relative wealth. As a minimum, any community needs to supply to its people retail trading outlets for groceries and hardware, service facilities for transportation and communication, agricultural services for supplying and maintaining equipment and also for marketing crops, health and welfare services, credit provisions, educational services, and social and recreational services.

This last category brings us to the church itself. What is the church life of the community? What should the churches be doing, and what are they in effect doing? To answer these and like questions we need to relate the membership and the participation in the churches to all the foregoing facts we have determined. Motive for a church and community survey begins in the church as it confronts its Christian responsibility, and the end of such a survey brings to the church an evaluation of its own effectiveness. Do the people who participate in the church come from all the areas of the community? Are all ages and categories of citizenry represented in the broad spectrum of church activity? Do leaders in the church come from all the segments of community life? We all have opinions or answers to these questions, but we need not depend upon opinion; we can count the people as they come to church and know the answers.

Out of these answers we shall be in a position to make recommendations to our churches and to the other agencies of community life, the recommendations evolving from our joint study. Such recommendations will not be superimposed upon the church members by an outside expert or an itinerant pastor; they will have grown out of the processes of the common life. In many communities, long before surveys have been completed, adjustments have been begun on the part of the constituent agencies and institutions of community life. If the citizenry are making the study, the study will have its immediate impact upon them.

Every survey effort should have as one of its concluding elements some provision for evaluation of the programs that grow out of the study; such an evaluation asks again and again the question: "Are the means we have selected for developing and changing our community and church producing the results we hope for or must we alter them in the light of experience?" A survey committee should raise early in the development of its work a special evaluation committee which will report back to the parent body at appropriate intervals. Such a committee can keep us from the disillusionment which so often overtakes churches and communities when their original effort to meet a problem revealed by their study leaves the situation it was intended to cure largely unchanged. If we envision this possibility and stand ready to apply correctives, disillusionment is avoided.

In professional circles it is the fashion nowadays to speak of continuing education. Preachers are never fully educated, they are always being educated, learning is an endless task. The same observation might well be made about churches and communities. The survey we have been discussing is never completed, it is always going on; basically we seek to establish such stances and habits of thought in the members of the church and citizens of the community to keep them in continuing and continuous learning. The rapidity of technological discovery and the mobility of persons in our society require continuous adjustment of institutions and agencies to the immediate shifting social situation. An occasional self-study is not enough; we need perennial and constant self-consciousness so far as our common lives are concerned.

In America prior to World War I, illiteracy was a real option; there was room in the common life for illiterates. Horses could be driven, ditches could be dug, crops could be planted and harvested, cows could be milked without benefit of reading ability. But today is different: illiteracy is no longer a viable alternative. He who cannot read the signs cannot drive on expressways; he who cannot read the map cannot tell where the expressway is taking him; the illiterate cannot even be sure in Chicago or Indianapolis of getting on the right bus. He who cannot read the instructions cannot assemble the new lawnmower or the baby buggy, and she who cannot read the instructions cannot even cook the cake in the cake-mix package. Reading has become a survival skill. Nor can churches any longer go it blind; they must have a sophisticated knowledge of the community in which they operate in order to operate at all. The survey is not an easy option; it is the alternative to institutional decay and death. A learning church is the only church that will survive in the change-riven late twentieth century. That is what the church and community survey is all about.

16

The Rural Church Changing the World

We began by indicating that our world is a world in change and that this fact of radical change is a constant to which the rural church and its pastor must respond. Yet we noted at the same time that the rural church is not externally an impressive institution: it is small in numbers in comparison with urban churches; its leadership is often part time and poorly trained; it tends to reflect the community life of which it is a part rather than bringing a leaven to that community life. The rural pastor operating in that kind of institutional setting may well regard the title of this chapter as hopelessly unrealistic and Utopian. After all, what can such a church do to change a world like ours?

Our answer to the question "What can the church

in fact do?" is essentially an answer built on faith. But sociological understanding can inform us as to the situation in which that faithful answer is to be given. We turn then to the question of what the future is to be for town and country people: specifically, what sort of community situation do current developments suggest as the challenge of the 1970s and 80s?

In chapter 1 we noted that modern man in America, as in all the developed countries, is affected by two factors: the continually accelerating supply of mechanical power available to the ordinary person, and the increasing mobility of persons as far as residence and occupation are concerned. Anxiety and alienation are the products of this situation in the person of the average man. We stand alone and afraid. Such loneliness and fear lead to a number of defensive postures —we referred to them as flights—which men and women of our day characteristically take. And one particularly dangerous posture is the projection of our fears on our unknown neighbor, seeing him as the threat that will engulf us, rather than sensing that the true threat is our own inner insecurity.

On the basis of this analysis, our possible future state lies between two polar extremes. On the one hand, power and mobility may accelerate our fears and alienation until, in one of the ever-more-frequent international incidents that characterize our instability, we make ultimate appeal to nuclear destruction. On the other hand, if we acknowledge the effects of power and alienation we may succeed in managing change, so that we realize for ourselves and all mankind the tremendous potential which exists in modern technology. The alternatives may be framed in the extreme of nuclear hell on the one hand and a physical heaven on the other.

Let us consider the alternative of atomic disaster first; if this is the fate of our civilization, then rural people are all that conceivably will remain when the clouds of nuclear dust have dissipated. And certainly not many of them will survive, only those sufficiently remote from metropolitan areas and out of the path of winds carrying nuclear contaminants; but they alone will remain. Their economic life will be one of crude subsistence, no more; their institutions will be impoverished or destroyed, but those who survive will require a ministry. Rural pastors will be needed to minister in their desperate situation.

In our technological culture so dependent upon the intricate interrelationships of modern industry, transportation, and communication, it is almost impossible for the imagination to envision the nature of human life in such a development. Our pioneer forefathers exploring the virgin wilderness of mid-America were better equipped to survive than we should be. Individual ability, ingenuity, and courage will be the qualities that make survival even thinkable. And the few survivors will turn to the town and country pastors who survive for guidance and courage. These men must be men of extreme imagination, patience, and sustaining vision. We are not in a position to help them very much in preparation for the ordeal of their leadership. All that we can suggest with any assurance is that town and country pastors and town and country churches now at work in rural America will be the sole bearers of Christian culture if and when atomic disaster overtakes us. They may not be the best qualified for the task but it will be their task; there will be no others left to carry the name of Christian.

But consider now the more happy alternative, that we manage to master and direct the change around us into a civilization which survives. What then of the rural pastor and his church? To this question we can give somewhat more discerning answers; in this latter case the shape of things to come lies before us. To begin with, it is safe to assert that there will be more people to be served by the town and country church and more for the pastor to do both absolutely and relatively than there is today. The very nature of the changes that we discuss in dealing with urbanization today guarantee that a large proportion of our populace will be rural tomorrow. These millions will be served in town and country churches by town and country pastors; the pattern of decentralization and weekend leisure may well mean that by the year 2000 there will be no one left in the great cities to attend church on Sunday unless it be visitors from the countryside bent on sightseeing. The weekend will be a time of flight from the city to the country. Indeed, the country, not the suburbs increasingly may become the living space and the family-rearing space of all our people.

To speak of these millions as "town and country" or "rural" is not to indicate that they will live in a world like town-and-country America now. From the cities they will bring with them conveniences, patterns of consumption, attitudes and interests which will make the rural world different. What will persist is the lower population density which differentiates rural from urban. The patterns of life they bring to town and country will have to be shaped to that population space factor.

The future, if we avoid disaster, will be marked by an increase in longevity, widely distributed wealth, and equally widely shared leisure. These trends, coupled with continued refinement and expansion in the fields of communication and transportation, will thrust people out into the countryside. The same forces which built the great suburbs of mid-twentieth century America will draw more and more people further and further away from the urban centers in their search for uncontaminated living space. Men will not be tied to their work for such long hours or for so long a working span. Under the same technological forces which continue to push down the hours of the working week, retirement will come earlier and earlier. Men and women will live to increasingly advanced ages with a degree of leisure that will place entirely new demands of programming upon the church and of service upon the ministry.

Such a population development will provide a stabilized and high-demand market for agricultural products. All of us will be able to eat and wear what we need and want; malnutrition and suffering from inadequate shelter will be unimaginable. There will be no agricultural surplus because ordinary Americans, and indeed, ordinary people the world around, will be able to buy the food and fiber they need. Farmers will not worry about price supports and quotas; they will produce in abundance because industry enables its workers to buy in abundance.

The farmers themselves will be a new type, fewer than ever before and incredibly more efficient in production and distribution. They will be technicians and specialists dealing expertly with single crops, taking full advantage of the latest mechanical inventions to utilize the most recent scientific discoveries. They will operate very large acreages very intensively; in this they will be aided and abetted by a corps of technical experts in seeds and soils, weed and insect control, agricultural engineering, veterinary science, and machine utilization and maintenance. The number of actual farm operators will decrease, while the para-agricultural population in rural areas will increase. All of these persons—farm operators and their technical assistants—will obviously be highly educated persons. The time is not far off when a degree in agriculture from an agricultural college will be a requirement for farm operation.

Concurrent with this specialization of agriculture will come the development of the countryside as living space. Modern transportation and communication systems make manufacturing decentralization not only feasible but economically advantageous; as factories wear out through normal obsolescence, they will be replaced by plants located outside of or marginal to the urban sprawl. And the same forces and facilities which enable manufacturing to be decentralized will make possible and encourage the dispersal of homes to the countryside. This involves not simply bringing city people to live in a small town or in the open country; it means bringing all the complex agencies which hitherto have characterized urban life pretty exclusively to the rural scene. Medical care systems, education on the junior college level and above, social agencies, both voluntary and governmental, will follow their constituents to rural residence. In doing so they will have to learn new techniques of service; their current practice built implicitly but unconsciously on the assumptions of high population densities will have to change to accommodate the new low population density pattern.

In consequence, new recreational land uses will develop across rural America. Already we are getting some feel for this in the national and state park systems, the camping movement, and the resort developments around our man-made lakes. Many, if not most, small towns throughout the middle west now have parks in which trailerites can remain overnight in their peregrinations across the country. But all these developments, and more as yet undreamed of, will accelerate as the total population of America becomes more rural in locale. The summation of the trends is simple: there will be more people living in rural America under conditions of low population density ten years from now than there are today; these people will share their living space for recreational use with the people still living in cities; all these people will have more leisure to invest; and on the pastor and the rural church will fall the burden of ministering to them in new and exciting ways.

Earlier, I contrasted the future possibilities as lying somewhere between *nuclear hell and physical heaven*.

It is probably clear to the reader that in the choice I favor getting the heaven if we can. But I would not want anyone to imagine that I am confusing the heaven about which I have been talking with the millenium or God's will on earth or the Kingdom of Heaven. God has put it in our range of possible achievement to order a world of plenty and peace and, I believe, his will is that we should work for such a world. But when that plenty and peace are achieved, men and women will still face the really significant questions of personhood. The hungry must be fed, the naked clothed, slavish toil must be banished, and crowded, contaminated, and contaminating housing be replaced; but when that achievement is complete we shall still need to deal with the loneliness of spirit that makes plenty and peace meaningless boredom. Jesus, in the parable of the Great Assize (Matthew 25:31-46), directs his judgment to men who apparently possessed adequate resources for feeding the hungry and otherwise ministering to human need. Their possessions did not save them; it was a difference in perception and attitude that distinguished the sheep from the goats, making one acceptable to the Judge and the other unacceptable.

Given a mastery of the physical ills of life tomorrow, what will then be the work of the churches and their pastors? I think the goal can be stated quite simply: the recovery of personhood. Men and women today feel lost in the mass: it is not just "small town in mass society," it is "little man in mass society." What men hunger for is a sense of individual meaningfulness, indeed the passion that drives many of us to

immerse our individuality in some social category is
the conviction that in so doing we shall discover and
realize our true nature. Black power, American power,
student power, union power, woman power, and "power
to the people" are all so many different anguished
appeals for recognition, dignity, independence, and
truly free selfhood.

In what way can the town and country church and
its pastor serve this fundamental need? The conditions of the town and country church and community
make them unusually effective protagonists of individual work, at least in potential if not in fact. If
people are to be persons they must discover themselves in small groups; the rural church and the rural
community are characteristically limited in numbers,
so that each person may be involved as an individual
with other individuals in common life. Contacts are
few enough so that we need not don our impersonal
protective mask to keep from being overwhelmed by
the burden of the hundreds assaulting sense and sensitivity on the "L" train or along the metropolitan
street. We can know all our neighbors in the small
town as we cannot know them in the suburban neighborhood or the high-rise apartment. The simpler structure and reduced numbers of rural life make the
personalization of all relationships a distinct possibility. That fact is one of the great advantages of the
town and country church.

Again rural heterogeneity of population is one of
the advantages of rural life. We certainly have heterogeneity in the city, but we deal with it in specialized
institutions, one function of which is to seal people

of a particular kind off from those who differ from them. Racial categories of citizens, economic levels, occupational groupings, and religious affiliations tend to herd together under urban conditions; there are enough of each kind in the heterogeneous mix of the modern metropolis so that each element to the mix can remain separate and in minimal relationship to all the others. No such social segregation is possible in the small community. We must all go to school and to church together; and this fact makes for a richer life for all as we draw on the heterogeneity of the citizenry to stimulate and enlarge our being.

And persons exist in town and country communities in manageable numbers: it is possible for us to know all our neighbors, to explore how each one feels in the face of a new problem or decision, to be aware of the tragedies that overwhelm each one and to minister in a direct, unmediated personal manner to the immediate personal tragedies of our brothers. I am not saying that we necessarily behave in this fashion in town and country communities and churches today; more often than not we fail to take advantage of the advantages that are ours. But I do insist that, whereas in areas of great population density it is impossible to be a person with every other human with whom we make contact, it is not impossible to do so in town and country life.

The work of the pastor and his people in town and country life tomorrow will be to help ordinary people to find and to share themselves with one another. Part of this comes through the preaching of the Word; "God so loved the world that he gave his only begotten

Son, that whosoever believeth in him should not perish, but have everlasting life." (John 3:16) Our acceptability before God is the first step in our discovery of our capacity to accept and to be accepted by one another. But there is much more than preaching to be done; indeed, it is probable that the effectiveness of our preaching will be based on the acting which persons observe in the church and in which they engage with the church.

By "acting" I mean simply that the church should become the instigator and sponsor of various programs in the community which bring ordinary people from all walks of the common life into relationship with one another. It does not greatly matter what these common activities are, indeed probably what they are will grow largely out of the particular local situation and the leadership talents available. In many communities a drama program is feasible and appropriate; in others the development of hobby groups is in line with need; in still others prayer groups or study groups that explore the meaning of our faith and experience are appropriate vehicles. Let me say that in my judgment a stamp collectors' group is just as functional in carrying out this aspect of the church's responsibility as a prayer group. What is significant is that persons are being helped to know one another on an intimate and uncontrived level under the auspices and in the spirit of the church.

In 1955 I was fortunate enough to participate in the World Conference on Rural Church and Community at the Ecumenical Institute, Chateau Bossy, Celigny, Switzerland. Among the delegates was Henry Randolph, longtime executive for town and country afffairs of the Presbyterian Church. In a discussion of the outreach of the churches in rural life, Dr. Randolph shocked the gathering by referring to "fish-fry evangelism." When pressed for an interpretation of the term, he told of a young Presbyterian minister in a seaside community who interested the men of his church in providing fish frys for the vacation visitors to the community through the summer months. The men—all the men of the community, not just the Presbyterians —caught the fish, cleaned and prepared them for the cooking, fried and served them to the hundreds of visitors who came week after week. In this common enterprise, men who had been virtual strangers to one another became friends and mutual confidants. Men in the community became proud of their manhood, their community, and their church. They began to understand by their participation in a common action what the church and its gospel were all about. Thus Dr. Randolph described "fish-fry evangelism."

Our European friends and some of the Americans and Asians engaged in a long criticism of this program: they decried it as theologically superficial and typically representative of American activism; they saw it as humanistic, removing all supernatural reference from the gospel and the church, taking God out of Christianity. But what they did not see was that this procedure enabled ordinary men to make a contribution to one another, to know one another both within and without the church as persons, and ultimately to receive what the church had uniquely to give to every one of them. And what they did not remember was that their Savior came originally to fishermen and challenged them, in a metaphor which they understood, to become "fishers of men."

Out of such simple interaction promoted by the church among its people, I should expect a new considerateness and tenderness to arise. The texture of our common life just now in America—both rural and urban—is brutal; no other adjective can describe it. We are engaged in violence abroad and there is a responding violence at home: threat and destruction are considered to be appropriate tactics in achieving "justice," which is interpreted in terms of what each particular group wants. We lack faith in one another and faith in ourselves, so we engage more and more in conduct growing out of our faith in force and violence. Someone, somewhere, must make a change, and the rural church and its pastor can make, in their manageable social setting, a beginning in the rebirth of simple kindness among men.

Can the rural church change the world; can so insignificant an institution in numbers, influence, and sophistication make any appreciable impact upon our mass society? My answer is a strong affirmative, not only because the rural situation is amenable to social change and management, but because our mass society is so hungry for the ministry that the rural church, if it will try, can bring. These chapters are written in the revolutionary hope that a new day will come in all America and in the whole wide world because of the faithful labors of the men and women whose glory is the town and country church.

Bibliography

CHAPTER 1—THE RURAL CHURCH IN A CHANGING WORLD

Copp, James H. ed. *Our Changing Rural Society: Perspectives and Trends*. Ames: Iowa State University Press, 1965.
    Sixteen key students in various sociological specialities bring analysis and prediction to bear on contemporary rural society, particularly in the West.

Taylor, Lee and Jones, Arthur R., Jr. *Rural Life and Urbanized Society*. New York: Oxford University Press, 1964.
    Two young scholars review systematically the status of the scientific understanding of our rural world. A textbook approach, but interesting and comprehensive.

CHAPTER 2—IS KNOWLEDGE POWER?

Smith, Rockwell C. et al. *The Role of Rural Social Science in Theological Education*. Evanston, Illinois: The Bureau of Social and Religious Research, Garrett Seminary, 1969.
    A report on the author's study of what rural sociolo-

gists think rural pastors ought to know, what rural pastors do know, and how their knowledge relates to their work in the church and community.

Thompson, Victor A. *Bureaucracy and Innovation*. Tuscaloosa: University of Alabama Press, 1969.

Is innovation possible in a bureaucratic organization? Thompson believes the development of professionalism in leadership will strengthen innovative possibilities.

CHAPTER 3—THE SOCIOLOGICAL PERSPECTIVE

Berger, Peter L. *Invitation to Sociology: A Humanistic Perspective*. Garden City, N. Y.: Doubleday and Co., 1963.

A thoughtful discussion of what sociologists try to do, by an expert craftsman among them.

Bertrand, Alvin L. *Basic Sociology*. Des Moines: Meredith Press, 1967.

This college text will bring the thinking of older students up to date; it is an excellent summary of the current sociological perspective in the U.S.A.

CHAPTER 4—NORMS AND VALUES

Cohen, Albert K. *Deviance and Control*. Englewood Cliffs, N. J.: Prentice-Hall, 1966.

Herein a sociologist points up the issues surrounding values and norms in American society. He is particularly helpful in outlining theory in the field for the layman.

Homans, George C. *The Human Group*. New York: Harcourt, Brace & World, 1950.

Groups are shown to produce norms in the on-going performance of everyday chores. The analysis is drawn from a careful exposition of classical group studies.

CHAPTER 5—THE COMMUNITY

Judy, Marvin T. *The Cooperative Parish in Nonmetropolitan Areas*. Nashville: Abingdon Press, 1967.

The modern knowledge of human ecology in rural areas is here applied suggestively to the work of the church.

Minar, David W. and Greer, Scott, eds. *The Concept of Community*. Chicago: Aldine Publishing Co., 1969.

Two scholars provide a selection of articles on the community from Thucydides and Aristotle through Thomas Paine and Charles Dickens to Ruth Benedict and William Golding. An excellent historical and contemporary introduction.

Sanders, Irwin T. *Community: An Introduction to a Social System*. 2nd ed. New York: Ronald Press, 1966.

A veteran rural sociologist here discusses community trends and issues on the basis of careful analysis and systematic understanding.

CHAPTER 6—THE POWER STRUCTURE

Mack, Raymond W. *Race, Class, and Power*. New York: D. Van Nostrand Co., 1968.

A collection of contemporary studies of various aspects of power in community: it relates community power to minority status and disabilities.

Rose, Arnold M. *The Power Structure: Political Process in American Society*. London: Oxford University Press, 1967.

A careful review of current studies and perspectives as to power in community and a reasoned presentation of the author's own theory and supporting facts.

Warner, W. Lloyd, Meeker, Marchia and Eells, Kenneth. *Social Class in America*. Chicago: Science Research Associates, Inc., 1949.

Here is a how-to book for the pastor who wants to make his own detailed analysis.

CHAPTER 7—COMMUNITY DECISION-MAKING

Kreitlow, Burton W., Aiton, E. W., and Torrence, Andrew P. *Leadership for Action in Rural Communities*. Danville, Illinois: The Interstate, 1965.

This volume is directed to the local leader in his community. The authors are educators in middle-west, east, and south.

Rogers, Everett M. *Diffusion of Innovations.* New York: Free Press, 1962.

A relatively up-to-date summary of the studies of the way persons adopt new practices.

CHAPTER 8—COMMUNICATION

Goffman, Erving. *The Presentation of Self in Everyday Life.* Garden City, N. Y.: Doubleday and Co., 1959.

The author expounds from his own participant observation and from various reports the devices adopted by persons, both individually and as teams, for presenting their self-image to outsiders.

Seifert, Harvey and Clinebell, Howard J., Jr. *Personal Growth and Social Change.* Philadelphia: Westminster Press, 1969.

A sociologist and a personal counselor join here to relate personality change to social change. Chapter 5 on "Communication that Facilitates Growth" is particularly helpful.

CHAPTER 9—ROLE

Glasse, James D. *Profession: Minister.* Nashville: Abingdon Press, 1968.

A pastor and teacher in a theological school prescribes a satisfying role understanding for pastors.

Hadden, Jeffrey K. *The Gathering Storm in the Churches.* Garden City, N. Y.: Doubleday and Co., 1969.

A professor of sociology analyzes the conflicting understandings of the minister's role which bring turmoil to contemporary church life.

Valdes, Donald M. and Dean, Dwight G. *Sociology in Use.* New York: Macmillan, 1965.

Chapter 3 contains helpful articles on "Role." Chapter

4 should be consulted in connection with our chapter on "Socialization" and chapter 2 with our discussion of "Culture." This is a good introduction to empirical sociology.

CHAPTER 10—SOCIALIZATION

Peck, Robert F. and Havighurst, Robert J. *The Psychology of Character Development*. New York: John Wiley & Sons, 1960.
Here the authors attempt to define character and to determine its genesis and development on the basis of youth studies in a midwestern community.
Ribble, Margaret A. *The Rights of Infants*. New York: Columbia University Press, 1943.
A physician analyzes the early needs of children and relates their satisfaction to subsequent personality developments.

CHAPTER 11—CULTURE

Herskovits, Melville J. *Man and His Works*. New York: Alfred A. Knopf, 1948.
This is a classic summary of the scientific achievements of cultural anthropologists. Twenty years have enlarged our knowledge but not materially altered the conclusions.
Lewis, Oscar. *The Children of Sanchez*. New York: Random House, 1961.
A contemporary anthropologist applies his science and art to the four children of a rural migrant to a Mexico City slum. The detail and objectivity make it a splendid example of cultural study.

CHAPTER 12—INTERACTION

Berger, Peter L., and Luckmann, Thomas. *The Social Con-*

struction of Reality. Garden City, N. Y.: Doubleday and Co., 1966.

Two scholars, one American and the other German, give attention to the theory of social knowledge and the central importance of interaction for social knowledge.

Blumer, Herbert. *Symbolic Interactionism: Perspective and Method*. Englewood Cliffs, N. J.: Prentice-Hall, 1969.

Here a major theorist in contemporary analysis offers a scholarly analysis of the concept of "interaction." Chapter 3 is particularly helpful.

CHAPTER 13—STATUS

Lasswell, Thomas E. *Class and Stratum*. Boston: Houghton Mifflin, 1965.

This volume summarizes research and theory regarding differential status in American society. The author draws on social psychology and political science as well as sociology to formulate his conclusions.

Slocum, Walter L. *Occupational Careers*. Chicago: Aldine Publishing Co., 1966.

A sociologist with wide experience in administration of vocational training and placement as well as teaching and research discusses the social concomitants of work and status in particular.

CHAPTER 14—THE CASE OF THE MISSING CONCEPT

Schaller, Lyle E. *Community Organization: Conflict and Reconciliation*. Nashville: Abingdon Press, 1966.

A pastor who is also a technically trained urban planner and who serves as director of a social research agency explores the literature of social conflict methodology for community change and offers a balanced appraisal.

Schermerhorn, Richard A. *Society and Power*. New York: Random House, 1961.

A sociologist looks at the conflicting powers of our

contemporary American society and gives social conflict
a theoretical setting.

CHAPTER 15—THE LEARNING CHURCH

Brewer, Earl D. et al. *Protestant Parish*. Atlanta: Com-
municative Arts Press, 1967.
    Sociologists and theologians combine to study and com-
pare a rural and an urban parish.
Hsin-Pao Yang, *Fact-Finding with Rural People*. Rome,
Italy: FAO Agricultural Development Paper No. 52.
August, 1955.
    The former head of the Rural Welfare Branch of the
Food and Agricultural Organization offers a simple out-
line for community study on a cross-cultural basis.
Note: Boards of national missions in many denominations
    have printed outlines for church self-study.
Stotts, Herbert E. *The Church Inventory Handbook*. Denver:
Wesley Press, 1952.
    A professor of sociology of religion explains alternate
approaches to the study of churches and communities and
offers clear and practical help.

CHAPTER 16—THE RURAL CHURCH CHANGING THE WORLD

Bell, David et al. *Ecumenical Designs*. New York: Steering
Committee, National Consultation on the Church in Com-
munity Life, 1967.
    A group of young church scholars speculate on the
future of the town and country church.
Mueller, E. W. and Ekola, Giles C. *Mission in the American
Outdoors*. St. Louis: Concordia Publishing House, 1966.
    Two Lutheran pastors and mission executives face the
challenge of the modern leisure and recreational develop-
ments to rural churches.
Noffs, Ted. *The Wayside Chapel*. Valley Forge, Pa.: Judson
Press, 1969.
    An account of an experimental metropolitan ministry

in Sidney, Australia, relevant here because it stresses
the imaginative approach to people and their needs, which
must characterize the church of tomorrow, rural as well
as urban.

Sills, Horace S. *Grassroots Ecumenicity*. Philadelphia:
United Church Press, 1967.

Here are six case studies of rural church experiments
ranging from rural New York to Montana. The emphasis
is on consolidation.

Index

208